BARCA PULITA

2 GE 5456 D

SO-AFX-699

SAILING AROUND THE WORLD
80 destinations

*To our friend, Fulvio Anzellotti, who found the time
before we left to accompany us to the pink-sand beach.*

WHITE STAR PUBLISHERS

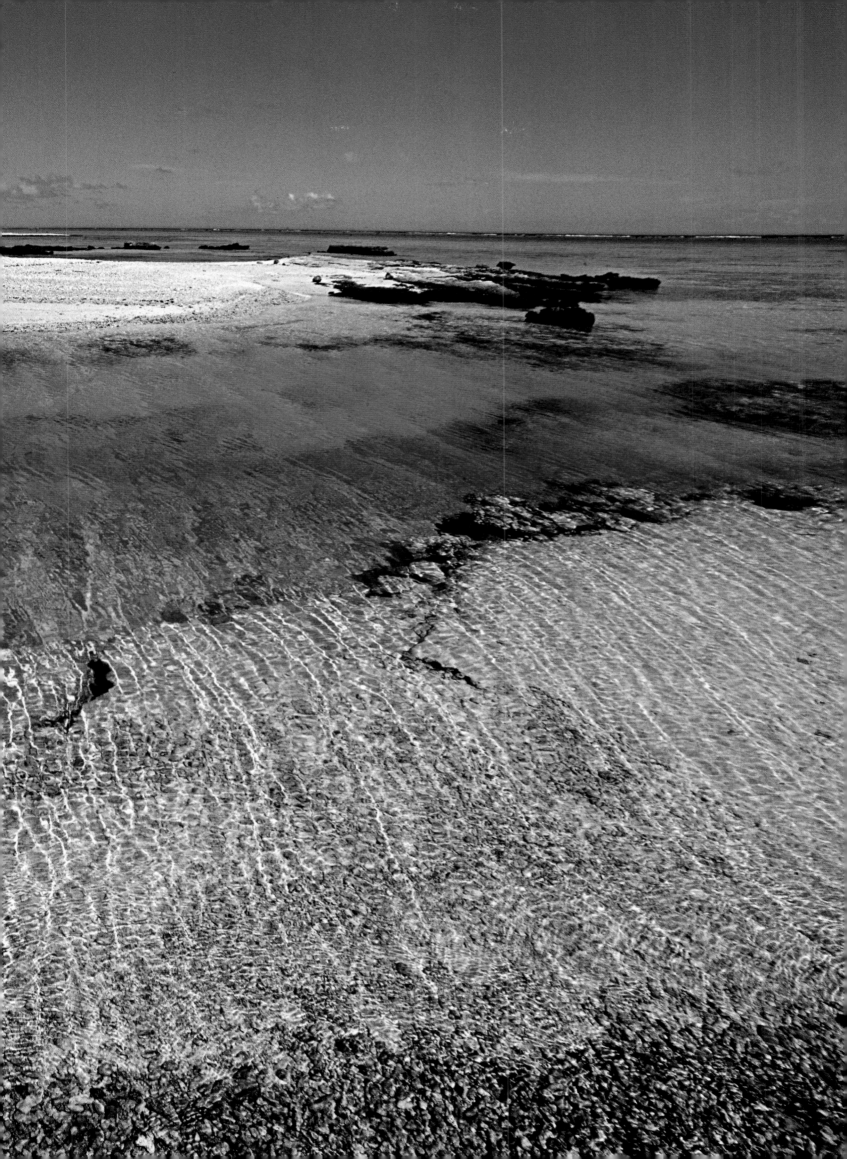

CONTENTS

TEXT
Elisabetta Eördegh
Carlo Auriemma

PROJECT EDITOR
Valeria Manferto De Fabianis

EDITORIAL COORDINATION
Laura Accomazzo

GRAPHIC DESIGN
Paola Piacco

1 The prow of the boat suspended over the turquoise water of a lagoon.

2-3 After weeks of sailing, a dark low line appears on the horizon.

4-5 The wonderful waters of Zanzibar.

6-7 The pass: a difficult and complicated route.

9 Over the course of our adventure, we used three different boats.

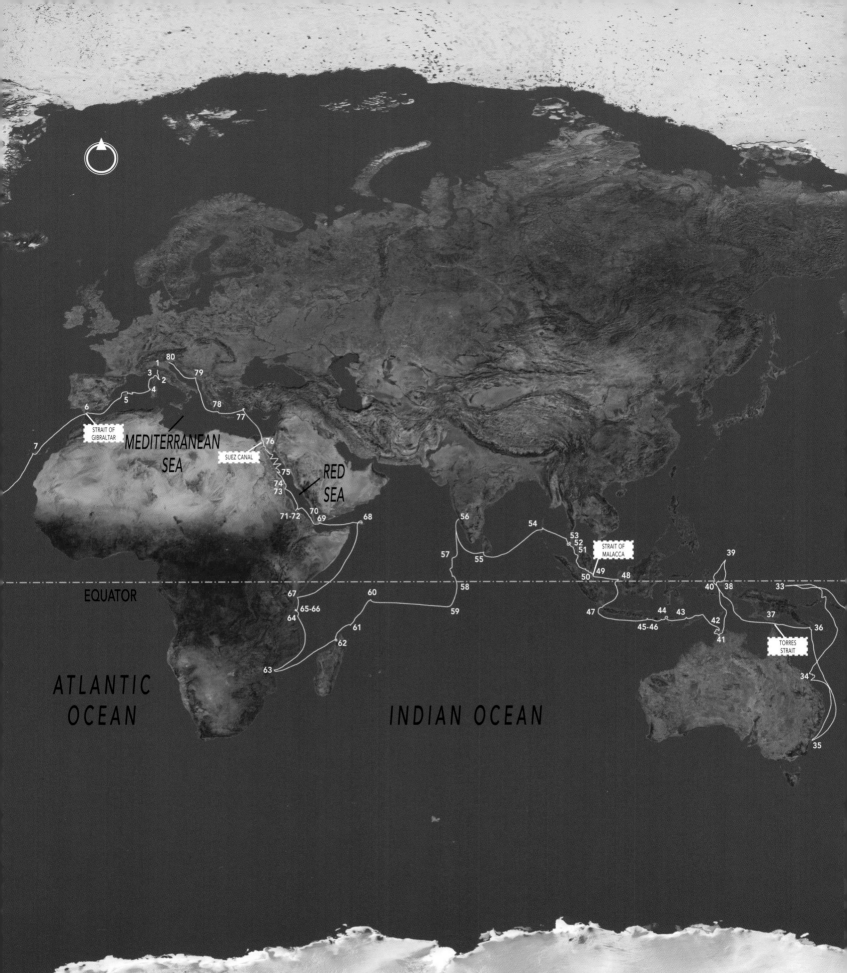

STRAIT OF GIBRALTAR

MEDITERRANEAN SEA

SUEZ CANAL

RED SEA

EQUATOR

ATLANTIC OCEAN

INDIAN OCEAN

STRAIT OF MALACCA

TORRES STRAIT

1. Porto Venere (Italy)
2. Monte Cristo (Italy)
3. Calvi (France)
4. Alghero (Italy)
5. Ibiza (Spain)
6. Gibraltar (United Kingdom)
7. Canary Islands (Spain)
8. Atlantic Ocean
9. Trinidad and Tobago (Trinidad and Tobago)
10. Los Roques (Venezuela)
11. Providencia (Colombia)
12. San Blas (Panama)

13. Panama Canal (Panama)
14. Cocos Island (Costa Rica)
15. Galapagos Islands (Ecuador)
16. Pacific Ocean
17. Marquesas Islands (French Polynesia)
18. Tuamotu Archipelago (French Polynesia)
19. Society Islands (French Polynesia)
20. Suvarov Atoll (Cook Islands)
21. Samoa Islands (Samoa)
22. Niuatoputapu (Tonga)
23. Phoenix Archipelago (Kiribati)

24. Tuvalu Islands (Tuvalu)
25. Quelelevu (Fiji)
26. Taveuni (Fiji)
27. Vatulele (Fiji)
28. Tanna (Vanuatu)
29. Ambrym (Vanuatu)
30. Anuta (Solomon Islands)
31. Vanikoro and Utupua Islands (Solomon Islands)
32. Marovo Lagoon (Solomon Islands)
33. Hermit Islands (Papua New Guinea)
34. Great Barrier Reef (Australia)

35. Sydney (Australia)
36. Samarai Island (Papua New Guinea)
37. Torres Strait
38. Irian Jaya (Indonesia)
39. Ayu (Indonesia)
40. The Moluccas (Indonesia)
41. Darwin (Australia)
42. Bathurst and Melville (Australia)
43. Lamalera (Indonesia)
44. Komodo (Indonesia)
45. Nusalembongan (Indonesia)
46. Bali (Indonesia)

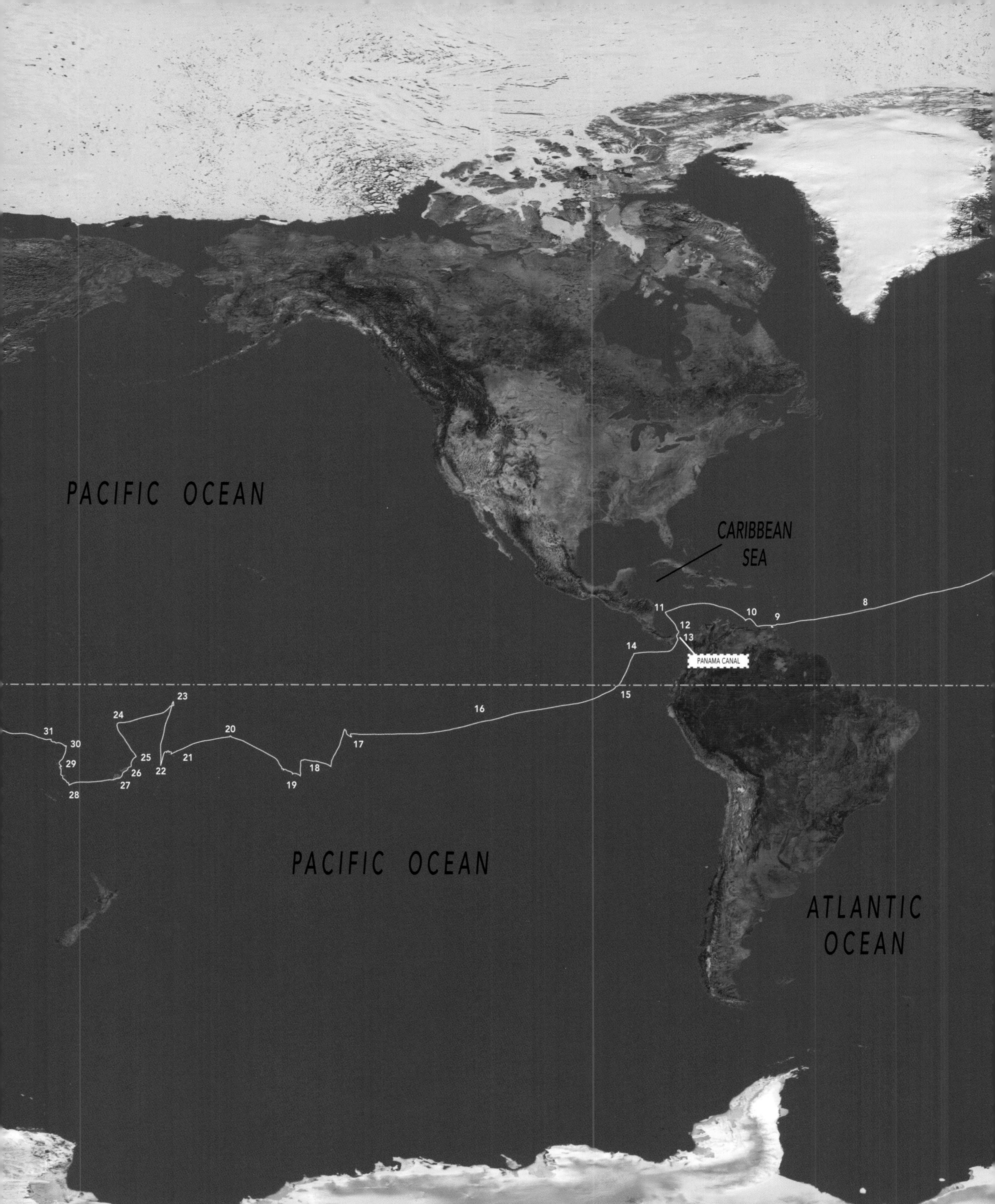

PACIFIC OCEAN
CARIBBEAN SEA
PANAMA CANAL
PACIFIC OCEAN
ATLANTIC OCEAN
8
9
10
11
12
13
14
15
16
17
18
19
20
21
22
23
24
25
26
27
28
29
30
31

47. Krakatoa (Indonesia)
48. Borneo (Indonesia)
49. Singapore (Singapore)
50. Strait of Malacca
51. George Town (Malaysia)
52. Panganga Bay (Thailand)
53. Surin Islands (Thailand)
54. Andaman Islands (India)
55. Galle (Sri Lanka)
56. Kochi (India)
57. The Maldives (Maldives)
58. The Great Equatorial Calms
59. Chagos Islands (United Kingdom)
60. Seychelles Islands (Seychelles)
61. Farquhar Atoll (Seychelles)
62. Nosy Komba (Madagascar)
63. Beira (Mozambique)
64. Mafia Island (Tanzania)
65. Zanzibar (Tanzania)
66. Latam (Tanzania)
67. Kilifi (Kenya)
68. Socotra (Yemen)
69. Aden (Yemen)
70. Hanish Islands (Yemen/Eritrea)
71. Dahlak Archipelago (Eritrea)
72. Massawa (Eritrea)
73. Suakin (Sudan)
74. The Marsas (Sudan)
75. Zabargad (Egypt)
76. Suez Canal (Egypt)
77. Rhodes (Greece)
78. Marmaris (Turkey)
79. Dubrovnik (Croatia)
80. Venice (Italy)

PREFACE

12-13 We begin our trip with one of the many small crossings that form part of the 40,000 miles (64,000 km) we will sail during our world tour.

13 left Filming, photographing, and writing are all ways to capture our emotions at the very moment when they occur, when they are at their strongest and most intense.

13 center Today's sails are cut out with a laser and sewn by machine, but if something tears in the middle of the ocean, we have to pick up a needle and thread and sew it by hand.

13 right Dolphins have fun swimming in the pressure surge that forms between the boat and the water, staying with us for hours, chasing us and swimming alongside our boat.

In this book, we describe our 80 Wonders of the World. Eighty sites that we selected according to our own very personal criteria among those encountered during 20 years of sailing through the oceans and along the coastlines of the world. Some of the spots we describe, such as the Maldives, Galapagos, Bali, and the Society Islands in the South Pacific, are extremely well-known, international tourist destinations, yet despite the annual arrival of millions of tourists, the beauty and fascination of these places remain intact, as well as their capacity

escape a cyclone, we entered a large bay then a river and a muddy dock, and here we had one of the strangest and most unusual experiences throughout our adventures. Facing the small island of Latam off the coast of Tanzania, we anchored with the idea of diving in to explore the seabed. In fact, we had to dive in and swim to the island because that was the only way to disembark and get an up-close view of that amazing piece of land covered by millions of squawking birds.

Some sites we selected are well-known wonders from

to touch the hearts and souls of those who visit them.

Other locations such as Anuta, Quelelevu, Ayu, and the villages along the Kapuas River in Borneo are unknown, difficult to reach, and by virtue of their remoteness from the civilized world have remained unspoilt. For us, they were marvelous gifts that we never expected to receive. Knowing we would find exceptional environments, the locations we intentionally sailed to include the Chagos Islands in the middle of the Indian Ocean, the Phoenix Islands in the central Pacific, and Anak Krakatoa in the Sunda Strait, which are distant lands difficult to reach, requiring complex navigation techniques, sometimes an extended time commitment and substantial effort. Our visits to these places involved incredible landings and anchoring in awkward spots, but we were repaid each time in a show of unique landscapes, provoking the strongest and most intense experiences that we could ever have imagined.

We reached other places by chance without having any idea of what was in wait for us, sometimes following directions from people we met along our journey, at other times dictated to by the weather. This is exactly what happened along the coast of Mozambique, where, to

a natural point of view, such as the Andamans, the *marsas* in the Red Sea, and Madagascar. Others were wonderful for the human encounters we had, for example, on Lamalera where for several months we accompanied the village men in their wooden boats when they went whale hunting, as they had done for over a 1,000 years, in Yakel on Tanna Island we collected images of the last traditional tribe of Vanuatu, and on Melville Island we were adopted by the Aboriginal community. We fondly recall all these encounters that encouraged us on our journey and sustained our enthusiasm to push on and to see what was beyond the next horizon.

Substituting Phileas Fogg's 80-day around-the-world challenge with our 80 wonders, we created a fantasy tour of the globe in a sailboat. It was a tour of the classical world, following tropical routes that left the Mediterranean by way of Gibraltar, crossing the three oceans with the trade wind, passing through the Panama Canal and the Torres Strait, and returning through the Red Sea back into the Mediterranean via the Suez Canal. We sailed through all these places and regions in our boat, although we did not land everywhere and chose to bypass some instead.

Inevitably, we had to set certain limits to our list of destinations. We decided to forgo the far north and the far south, and sacrificed all temperate zones outside the Mediterranean. This meant that we remained in the warmer and milder climates of the tropical belt. We were very laidback and avoided the strenuous effort required to tackle difficult sailing through bad and cold weather, choosing instead to be always blanketed in heat and humidity. For us, the sea is what we had dreamed of during winter as children: warmth, sunlight, and bathing suits.

This book is quite different to those we have written thus far. It is a book that tells our stories in photographs with accompanying, small diary passages. The intention is to provide snapshots of our experiences; personal moments, physical and emotional, of our encounters with each location. Naturally, the sailing perspective in the images is a very privileged one. Over the course of all our voyages, we changed boats three times. The first, *Il Vecchietto (Little Old Man)* was an Alpa 11.50 manufactured in Italy and which carried us on our first

Some of our stopovers on this fantastic journey were obligatory: Gibraltar, the Torres Strait, and the Panama and Suez canals. These are iconic points that everyone must pass at some stage when undertaking long-distance voyages. The passing through of so many travelers has affected the native peoples along these routes and modified their traditions. However, there are still places where you can sense something of what the great explorers of the past must have felt when they first encountered some of the world's most celebrated locations during the age of the voyages of discovery.

world tour from 1988 to 1991. The second, *Mastropietro (Master Peter)* was a 49-ft (15-m) schooner, which was also built in Italy and inaugurated our Green Boat project, departing from Porto Venere in 1993 and arriving on the east coast of Australia seven years later. There we found our current boat, *Gioia Levu (Joy of Levu)*, a Rorqual 44 constructed in France at the Nautical Saintonge shipyards. We are still sailing in it today as we continue the journey of our Green Boat project. All three boats appear in this book.

E. Tödeli
Carlo Auriemma

14 left *Calculating distance on the nautical map with a compass is an antiquated but still accurate practice.*

14 center *Bronzed skin, neglected hair, and a frayed flag are all signs of being at sea for a long time.*

14 right *To our delight and within range of our lenses, marine birds stop and nest on many distant islands.*

15 *Being at the rudder in a calm and protected bay with a welcome breeze is one of the most pleasurable times to sail.*

INTRODUCTION

The sailboat is a wonderful means of transportation because it allows people to reach otherwise inaccessible locations and to do it following the slow, natural rhythms of the sea and wind. You leave, sailing for days, sometimes even weeks, until land finally appears, and that new and unknown land may at times result in unexpected encounters, offer new discoveries and vistas, and inspire intense emotion.

We were not aware of all this when we left the wharf at Porto Venere, Italy, 20 years ago for our first world tour in a sailboat. We were leaving on an adventure for ports of call we could not even imagine, only intending to take a sabbatical, a break from a more or less normal life, and from our conventional but gratifying work. This tour was planned to last two years and actually took three, but in retrospect we would have preferred it to be longer. These were three years during which we found ourselves lost in the vast space of the oceans, traveling over enormous distances, landing on unknown coastlines, arriving at islands where the people neither had running water nor were familiar with the concept of money or the stresses of modern civilization. We experienced bad weather as well as the enchanting calm of atolls with long, pristine beaches and not a human footprint in sight. We had encounters with natives, cultures, and customs that we didn't even know existed.

Upon our return to Italy after three years and 40,000 miles (64,000 km), we had changed profoundly. Our boat brought us back home but our hearts and minds remained there in those distant worlds, in those previously unknown realities of which we had only caught a glimpse. Back home, we began to fit back into the life we had lived before, meanwhile holding onto our memories and impressions by recounting our adventures to others and describing our encounters. We created a book from those memories and to our surprise people enjoyed it, and the published book became the impetus for a series of articles and some television appearances. We told the story of how one night, off the coast of Colombia, we became extremely frightened upon seeing a suspicious boat, recounted how we were introduced to the prime minister of Fiji, and described our first sighting of the green flash on the open sea. So many people enjoyed our stories and observations that a radically life-changing idea came to light. Why not take off again and devote a new voyage to document, photograph, and film the unspoilt environments, the traditions that were being lost, and the peoples who were dying out? After all, the earth is enormous and diverse, full of so many different peoples just waiting for us to tell their stories. This is how our Green Boat project came to life.

Sailboats in general are an ecological means of transport, but the Green Boat would be even more so. We would install solar panels and a wind-driven generator in order to use only renewable energy sources, not to depend on the motor to run everything on board, and to experiment with non-toxic antifouling and other non-polluting products. Once we found a large enough boat, we equipped it according to these criteria and in less than two years we were ready to leave. We ventured forth, this time without establishing any deadline for returning, yet with a pre-planned route to follow. The world stood before us with the promise of new adventures and stories to collect, we were undaunted and ready to throw ourselves into pursuit of that enormous endeavor, to go and search

16-17 Few things are as difficult to photograph as the boat you are sailing yourself and fortunately every once in a while we could count on skilled friends.

17 top left The rudder wheel is the boat's helm and steering mechanism, yet luckily we can rely more on the wind rudder to maneuver it.

17 top right Il Vecchietto (The Little Old Man), the Alpa 11.50 that carried us on our first world tour from 1988 to 1991: 40,000 miles (64,000 km), three oceans, and five continents.

out the most beautiful and still pristine places remaining in the forgotten corners of the globe.

Once we left the Mediterranean, we lost ourselves in the crystal waters along the uninhabited coasts of the Red Sea, one of the most fascinating environments in the world, then we encountered the Horn of Africa, the Socotra and Chagos archipelagos, and Madagascar. In just a few months, we had already collected tales from shark fishermen on the Hanish Islands, our first images of the Dahlak and Eritrea islands, once again accessible after 30 years of civil war, and learnt about the tuna fishermen of the Maldives, the great sailing *dhows* of Zanzibar, and the sapphire miners in Sri Lanka. Thus began our first series of short bulletins from the Green Boat, with accounts of our seemingly insignificant yet intriguing encounters. After three years, we finished a second book, after just four our first documentary was broadcast, and today after 15 years our wanderlust still hasn't been satisfied.

18 top Strenuous sailing sometimes repaid us with spectacular and unique sights, and with the strongest and most intense reactions that we could ever have imagined.

18 bottom In 1993, we departed once again on the Mastropietro *(Master Peter), a 51-ft (15-m) schooner that carried us for seven years across the Red Sea, the Indian Ocean, all the way to Australia.*

19 This is our current boat, the Gioia Levu (Joy of Levu), a Rorqual 44 built in France at *the Nautical Saintonge shipyards. We bought it in Australia from a German world traveler.*

20-21 Sunset is the best time of day, the wind calms, the water becomes still, and the light creates wonderful effects.

> *We depart escorted by all of the boats in the port, leaving them behind, one by one, until we find ourselves alone facing the vast, empty, and indifferent sea.*

Porto Venere

THE GULF OF POETS

The Gulf of Poets was our training ground and our refuge. In all sorts of weather, in every season, we would arrive in the middle of the night at Le Grazie, walk down the steep path, find our old dinghy, and row out to the boat. While on many a winter night we would pass ferries anchored at the big black buoys across from Palmaria, and there were always so many glistening mussels attached to the buoys! Then there were the days when we docked at the wharf at Porto Venere, waiting for the rain to stop and the crashing breakers to calm, with the pastel building façades in the old village shiny and dripping wet overlooking a sea as silver as mercury. On other occasions we would walk back up the Carugio path with our heads lowered against the southwesterly winds, climbing up to the little church of Saint Peter to get a good viewpoint to see the waves beating against the rocks below and the larger waves in the sea beyond against that grey yet still inviting horizon. When summer started and the sea began to get crowded, there were so many places where we could again find refuge: Palmaria, Lerici, Fiascherino, Tellaro, the friendly yet unreliable little port of Magra, and, further west, the marinas at Cinque Terre. Not forgetting the shipyard at Bocca di Magra that was our home during the long months passed preparing the boat. So many weekends spent stripping, varnishing, cutting, and sewing, all under the watchful, benevolent, and amused eyes of those who knew how to do those tasks much better than we did. And, of course, the Tino lighthouse that welcomed us home again after our short or long cruises.

Our voyage could not start from anywhere else but from here, from this wonderful corner of the world, this little old village where we live. The village owes its existence to the rocky cliff which gave it such an intimate relationship with the sea, entwining its history with that of the Mediterranean in a splendid fushion of truth and legend. Its own name, perhaps owing to its beauty or perhaps to the temple of Venus that was erected above the church of St. Peter, recalls the foamy sea where the goddess was born. The sight of Porto Venere moving away in the distance is still in our hearts. Many times in the middle of an ocean or waiting to land on some distant coast in that vast unchanging body of water, we would think, and still do, almost for luck, how much we missed sighting the Tino lighthouse welcoming us back home.

22-23 Legend has it that on the rock of St. Peter's church there was a temple dedicated to the goddess Venus Erycina, from which the name Porto Venere derived.

22 bottom and 23 bottom right Before departure the last work is completed on the Green Boat, as neighboring mariners celebrate our accomplishments.

23 bottom left The Green Boat leaves the pier at Porto Venere for its inaugural voyage, heading first to the Tuscan archipelago.

24-25 Today's Calata Doria pier was constructed over the rocks that women of Porto Venere say were sprinkled with tallow to prevent pirates from landing here.

23

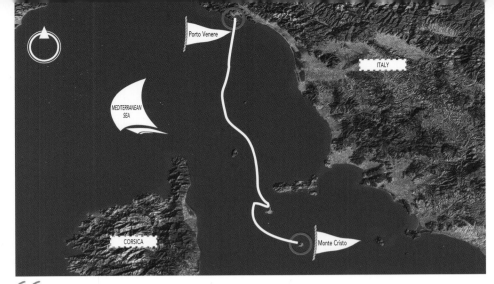

150 Miles. Two days and one night among the islands of the Tuscan Archipelago to reach Edmond Dantes' refuge, now a kingdom of marine birds and wild goats.

Monte Cristo

LITTLE PEARL IN THE TYRRHENIAN SEA

Was Alexandre Dumas ever here? Or if when he sent Edmond Dantes to the island to follow Abbot Faria's orders, was he speaking from personal experience? Who knows if he ever saw the subterranean caves where the Count of Monte Cristo decorated his luxurious residence with dark oriental rugs. It is a fact, however, that Monte Cristo has changed very little since it was described by Dumas in his book. A rough diamond implanted in the sea, a rugged mountain that rises up from the cobalt blue, with sparse vegetation that does not successfully hide the gray and pink granite of which it is formed. The island is difficult to land on and walk around, and was home for centuries only to hermit monks that shared the mountain with wild goats and colonies of birds. Then in the year 800 it became a hunting preserve of the House of Savoy and consequently ordinary folk were not allowed to set foot on the island. Today, it is a nature park, a preserve where only a watchman and his family live, along with two forest rangers, who alternate every two weeks.

Monte Cristo is the first stopover on our voyage and before losing ourselves in the oceans, we decide to stop here as a kind of pilgrimage to one of those few Mediterranean spots that has preserved a semblance of natural equilibrium. Dropping anchor at Cala Maestra is tight but secure. On land just above the bay, there are just a few trees and the old walls of the royal villa that today is the residence of the watchman and rangers. The rest is nature in its purest state, rugged and wild. The sea beats violently against the rocks and enters the mouths of the many caves at sea level. There are also other caves just above the shoreline and further up the cliffs. The existence of these caverns fueled the centuries-old legends of hidden treasures – donations hoarded by the monks, the loot from pirate raids, and inheritances brought here by envious relations – all hidden in the secret places of the island to safeguard against further plunder.

The steep and rocky old mule track leads upward to the area known as the Monastery, where the ruins of the old building still remain. The effects of the voraciously grazing wild goats over the centuries can be seen everywhere as they have dramatically modified the growth and distribution of the original Mediterranean scrub. The breezes carry the fragrances of thyme, rosemary, and the sea. Seen from above, the boat is a white dot in the middle of a blue pool and the only sound is that of the wind among the bushes below. Humans do not seem to be a part of this solitary world, remaining just as it is, strangely untouched, right in the middle of the very crowded Tyrrhenian Sea.

26 bottom Rising from the cobalt blue, a high mountain with sparse vegetation that can't mask the gray and pink granite of its peaks.

26-27 The Green Boat rests at Cala Maestra, the only anchorage in this solitary world, remaining strangely intact in the middle of the very crowded Tyrrhenian Sea.

27 bottom The old, steep, and stony mule track leading upward to the area called the Monastery, where the ruins of the old monastery still stand.

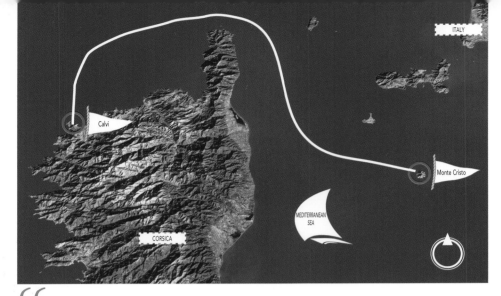

150 Miles. Two days heading west around Cape Corsica, crossing an invisible border, and landing in France at the foot of a citadel with evocative scents and echoes of ancient times.

Calvi

THE CITADEL

alvi is a magnificent natural harbor, a completely protected body of water, and the ideal spot to rest after our first short crossing and straighten out any problems in anticipation of what seems to be a storm, but perhaps it will be just a very windy night. Around us is an old village with houses that have been home to generations of sailors and its narrow winding streets full of shops offering a kaleidoscope of scents and flavors, which we've not yet experienced but will miss in the coming months. The narrow winding streets rise towards the Genovese citadel towering over the port, the village, and the coastline. It was from its walls that invaders' ships were sighted and behind its ramparts the villagers barricaded themselves when lower defense outposts had been

taken. However, we do not perceive the magnitude of what surrounds us. Our thoughts are more with the future, imagining the new seas and distant lands we are about to experience. We are focused on getting to know our boat and the way it works, on planning routes, and on learning how to use the navigational equipment. For us, the citadel becomes the ideal post to practice making observations with the sextant, the tool that should guide us across the oceans.

Each morning towards 11 a.m., we walk through the narrow lanes to reach the small square and then upward onto the ancient walls to get a good view of the sea. Sitting on the overhanging rock, we point the sextant, orienting the mirrors and begin to measure the height of the sun in minutes as it rises and the angle increases slowly from 49° 21′ 30″ then to 49° 21′ 36″, and so on and so forth until the moment arrives around midday when the sun seems to stop in the middle of the sky. Its height no longer increases, the sun remains suspended immobile as if time has stopped. It is the moment when the meridian altitude aligns with the sun. A handful of seconds pass and then the sun resumes its path, now lowering to the horizon. And we also rush downward along the sunny alleyways to the boat where the quick reference tables and the little book of directional instructions await us, explaining the mysteries of astronomical navigation. The sun descends from the meridian of high noon and, through a series of calculations and corrections, we must determine our latitude. At our first attempt, our meridian puts us in the southern hemisphere. We try again the next day and it goes better but our results indicate that we are just north of Tunisia. On the third day the meridian put us two miles south of Calvi. This is an acceptable error and means that we have learned something. Certainly, it will be more difficult in the ocean because waves will break the horizon and the tossing sea will make observations fleeting, but those are things that we will learn to deal with over time, day after day, in the open sea.

28 bottom Measuring the height of the sun over the horizon with the sextant, making calculations and consulting the charts, we are able to trace a straight line that passes through our location.

29 In the waters around the long promontory of Cape Corsica, you can sail through one part of the Mediterranean where it is relatively common to encounter whales and dolphins.

30-31 *From the walls of the citadel, attacking ships were sighted and enemies were held off when the defenses below had been overcome.*

31 top *A splendid natural anchorage along the coast of western Corsica where the colors of the sea are incredible, contrasting with sun-scorched, sparse vegetation.*

Calvi

31 center The profile of the old Revellata lighthouse dominates the wild and rocky bay by the same name, just west of Calvi.

31 bottom The old village of Calvi rises up on the promontory projecting over the sea, a wide port dominating the entire bay and safely sheltering sailboats.

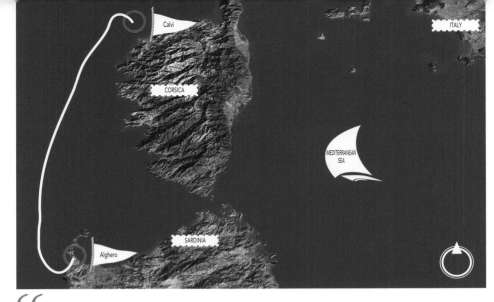

" *150 Miles. Another two days of crossing an invisible border to return to Italy, to a place that already suggests Spain.* "

Alghero

SPRINGBOARD FOR DEPARTURE

It is a distance of 215 miles (345 km) from Alghero to the Balearic Islands, a relatively short journey compared to the distances that we will cover in the following months, but the furthest voyage we have made so far. It will only be a two- or three-day crossing but we have never been in the middle of the sea for so many days without land in sight and no points of reference in view. We will have to pay attention to the compass because the Balearic Islands are small and if we are just 10° off course we could miss Minorca. Also, since the Balearic Islands are aligned one after the other, if we do not sight Minorca then we won't be able to sight the other islands, and might risk continuing on towards who knows where. Fortunately, the mountains of Minorca are high and if the sky is clear, we will be able to sight it from a distance. In case of any difficulty, the most powerful radio beacon in the Mediterranean is on Mount Mahon, and we will most assuredly pick up its signal. We have a radio and antenna on board, although as yet we have not used them.

This is what was at the back of our minds as under the benevolent watch of our old village we spent our days finalizing preparations on the boat for this our first small, yet momentous, crossing. We checked and rechecked the shackles, rigging screws, stay adjuster and turnbuckles, the rudder lines, and propeller log. We practiced with the sextant and, in addition to the meridian, we now know how to calculate the celestial fix. We have become familiar with the rudder wind controls that should alleviate our turns at commanding the boat. We will take three-hour shifts then trade off with whoever has slept for the previous three hours, spending three hours on the well deck standing watch as we sail then switch posts. When we finally decide to leave, it is sunset and the sun sets the sea on fire before us beyond the boat's prow. We hope that this trail of fiery water will lead us to the mountain elevations on Minorca in three days time.

We anticipate a wind from the southeast of between 10 and 15 knots (11–17 m.p.h.). To us, that means beautiful weather and a moderately calm sea.

32 bottom Navigating for days in the midst of the sea without land or any other points of reference in sight, you must find the winds to carry your sails.

33 We begin to forget our old village streets, churches, squares, and shops, they are just things of the recent past that will be missed from afar.

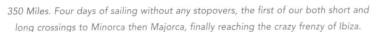

> 350 Miles. Four days of sailing without any stopovers, the first of our both short and long crossings to Minorca then Majorca, finally reaching the crazy frenzy of Ibiza.

Ibiza

AN ENDLESS PARTY

Minorca is the first island, tranquil and a bit English. Then there's Majorca, more Spanish and busier, attracting both the general public and elite with its Copa del Rey regattas. But, when we sight Ibiza, still off the coast, we understand that we are going into a different world. On Ibiza, you can immerse yourself in the alternative and unrestrained world of pleasure, of parties and nightclubs, or find yourself anchoring off the coast in total isolation and peace. You may spend your days in complete solitude on the rocks, collecting snails and limpets, then an evening in a noisy, vibrant crowd, going deaf from the loud music. Ibiza is the island for enthusiasm, excess, and perpetual partying.

Entering the old port of Sa Penya, we unwittingly become involved in this perpetual party and never emerge from it during the entire time we spend on the island. People, music, and dancing every evening and every night, in a continuous crescendo until we arrive at the mother of all parties, the *Locura*

de *Verano*, where the frenzied crowd dresses up and pours out into the alleys of the old village. There are performance artists on stilts, acrobats, fire-eaters, and dancing and singing until the first light of dawn. Anything is allowed in this pagan celebration that kicks off the start of summer and celebrates the wildness sparked by its arrival and the climate of freedom and tolerance that permeates Ibiza throughout the rest of the year, inducing a carefree attitude, lightheartedness, and, yes, euphoria.

Our keel pays for this state of euphoria the next day when deciding which route to take across the channel between Ibiza and Formentera. There are three possible routes. The nautical chart states that the first is only for rowboats, the second for somewhat larger watercraft, while the third is good for ships, ferries, and sailboats. Inebriated by the uber-relaxed atmosphere and rendered optimistic by a gin and tonic consumed too early before sunset, we opt for the route that saves in distance and time. The sea is calm, the route deserted, and we are enveloped in a cloud of magical unreality. Just when we think we are beyond any tricky situation, something suddenly shakes the boat, a jolt that makes the hull tremor and the masts vibrate. We look at each other, amazed and incredulous, as the keel has evidently collided with a rock on the seabed. Another jolt follows then yet another. Our blood runs cold, turning around is impossible as is stopping and we can only carry on very slowly, expecting the worst to happen from one moment to the next. There is another thud then a long scraping sound, a sign that the seabed is sandy, and finally silence with just the slight sound of the hull sliding into deeper waters. We come out of it "bruised," but nevertheless we consider ourselves lucky not to have lost the boat.

This is how our first boat rule comes into play: never drink alcohol while sailing!

34-35 Ibiza is the island for enthusiasm, debatable behavior, and perpetual partying, where every evening you may immerse yourself in a colorful crowd, a climate of freedom, and permissiveness.

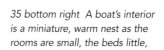

35 bottom right A boat's interior is a miniature, warm nest as the rooms are small, the beds little, and the galley is tiny, but when confronting the open sea it is a welcome home away from home.

34 bottom and 35 bottom left Around the coast of the island you can still find solitary spots where you can anchor and spend your days away from the crazy crowds of partygoers.

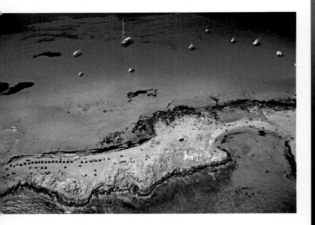

36 and 36-37 Although we are still in the Mediterranean Sea, the turquoise tints and transparency of the sea around Formentera are equal to those found in the tropics.

Ibiza

38-39 In 1713, Spain ceded to Great Britain "full and entire ownership of the city and castle of Gibraltar in perpetuity, without exception, or impediment of any kind."

38 bottom left The lighthouse on Gibraltar rises up where Calpe stands tall, one of the Pillars of Hercules, as we leave it in our wake, anxiously entering the vastness of the Atlantic.

38 bottom right Signaling infectious disease and quarantine in the past, the yellow or Q flag is now raised to mark passage into a new country.

39 bottom Schools of dolphins play in the waters of the strait, attracted by the current that flows between the Atlantic and the Mediterranean which inverts four times a day.

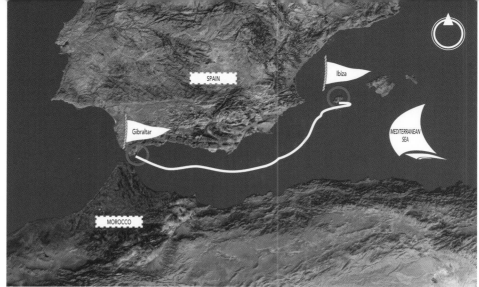

" *450 Miles. It takes five days with uncertain winds over the Alboran Sea to reach this strange rock next to Spain where the United Kingdom still governs.* "

Gibraltar

THE PILLARS OF HERCULES

The officials that come aboard to check the boat and our documents have on short shorts and thick knee-length socks. They only speak English and behave according to that pompous etiquette that just a few miles away on the coast of Spain no one would dream of employing. They complete their procedures and before leaving, invite us to lower the Q Flag or the yellow flag, never used in the Mediterranean, welcome us to Gibraltar, and give us permission to proceed to the yacht club. And here in the modern and well-equipped marina, everything is impeccably English. In the shop, they sell souvenirs with images of Queen Elizabeth, tabloid newspapers, horse and gardening magazines, and Penguin books. Just a few dozen yards further in Spain, are markets with stalls full of melons, peaches, apricots, fresh fish and shrimp that are still jumping, cow and goat cheeses, hams, whole loafs of bread and baguettes, and oil. In Gibraltar, there are no markets, just efficient and immaculate supermarkets that offer potatoes, rhubarb and green apples, cheddar and blue cheeses, salted butter and margarine as well as vacuum-packed bacon, chutney, mince pies, and an infinite supply of savory pies made with mutton, lamb, and beef. It is as if you are no longer in sunny southern Spain, but in some port on the south coast of England. It is from here, from this ancient rock of contention between Spain and Britain, that our voyage really begins. Passing through the Pillars of Hercules, we leave the warm protective waters of the Mediterranean that we have known since we were kids, where we learned to swim, to love the sea, and to sail. The *Mare Nostrum* ("Our Sea") surrounded by so many countries with their friendly people, familiar languages, and delicious cuisines. Everything beyond the Mediterranean will be different, great distances to be covered, strong winds, raging currents, and perhaps even storms await us. A bigger

world altogether, a new way of handling the wind in our sails (or not), and a sailing experience that excites and motivates us yet strikes fear in our hearts and makes us feel uneasy. We leave the strait and for the first time in our brief careers as sailors we have to seriously consider the strong and sudden current whose center runs towards the ocean as the leeward coast pushes us from the other side, changing from hour to hour and inverting four times per day. There are lanes for ships entering the Mediterranean and for those exiting towards the Atlantic. There are ferries going to and from the Spanish and African coasts. The traffic is both daunting and impressive. For us, who are small and awkward, there is nothing else to do but maneuver into wind gusts with favorable currents where the traffic allows. After 10 hours of agonizing concentration, everything gets smoother, the current abates slowly, the coastline moves away in the distance, and the traffic clears. We suddenly find ourselves alone for the first time on the ocean with the Portuguese trade wind in our sails.

39

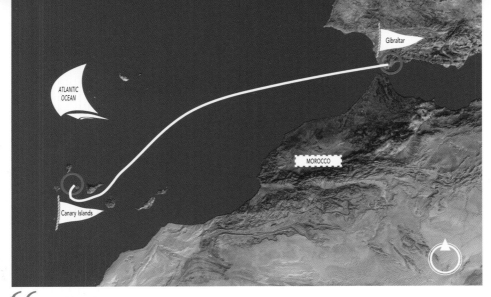

> 750 Miles. Ten days pushed along by the Portuguese trade wind and then a stopover, as Columbus did, at these distant islands in anticipation of making the great crossing over the Atlantic.

The Canary Islands

COLUMBUS' POINT OF DEPARTURE

Christopher Columbus, the great navigator and explorer, began his crossing at the Canary Islands. As history states, the great voyage actually began at Palos where the Admiral set sail with his three caravels heading for the Indies, but the first leg was brief, just as far as the Canary Islands (La Gomera). The stopover was due to the necessity of loading fresh water, firewood, wine and to visit the woman with whom Columbus was in love. From a technical viewpoint, the stopover was essential. From these islands in the middle of the ocean, where winds were blocked by the mountains and blew into the channels between the islands with unexpected force, the navigator could head out into that unexplored ocean hoping to prove that he could reach the Spice Islands (East Indies) by sailing in that direction. From the Canary

Islands, he could sniff the air and determine whether the trade wind had stabilized, whether thunderstorms were coming from Africa, whether that combination of sea, air, and sky, which were so important to navigating, was favorable for his departure. Just like Columbus and so many others who came before, we are also leaving from the Canary Islands. The island where we lingered to sniff out the trade winds and sea conditions was that of Tenerife, in the bay of Los Gigantes, along with many other boats, all intent upon preparing for a voyage to the Antilles. Our pre-departure to-do list is long but the one item that jumps out at us is stocking the pantry! This is our first oceanic crossing, we don't know how to behave, how to preserve fresh food without a refrigerator, we don't know how to determine quantities of rations, how long the voyage will take, and we don't even know if we are good fishermen! Other crews have the same issues and our conversations with them when we meet always revolve around recipes, names of shops, and advice on what to buy. There are various schools of thought on how to preserve eggs. There are those who cover them with Vaseline, those who store them in ashes, those who parboil them for a minute, or those who preserve them like one does fish, in glass containers filled with oil after boiling them, or drying them in the sun after dusting them with salt. There are also many theories surrounding fresh produce and the one that comes up the most frequently is a method of preserving bananas. You have to peel them, cut them in long slices, dry them in the sun then put them back into paper bags. The experts say that they will last for months this way. Bananas are grown commercially in the Canary Islands, green bunches are picked from trees and, once completely identical and calibrated, are packed, loaded onto refrigerated ships, and sent to Europe. Bananas that are too long, short, misshapen, or too ripe are rejected and left in huge piles in the sheds. It is customary for sailors to tour the packing facilities and collect any discards. *"Come con salud!"* were their good wishes as we leave the banana packers.

40 bottom Blocked by the mountains, the Portuguese trade wind flows over the channels between islands with unexpected force, making sailing difficult.

40-41 The Canary Islands are a strategic spot to wait for the trade wind to stabilize and for the right combination between sea, wind, and weather before departing.

41 bottom left Thanks to the convenient footholds on the mast, you can easily climb up to the crosstree to check the topmast shrouds.

41 bottom right A coating of Vaseline spread uniformly over eggs seals the porous shells, allowing you to preserve them longer in the heat and humidity on board the boat.

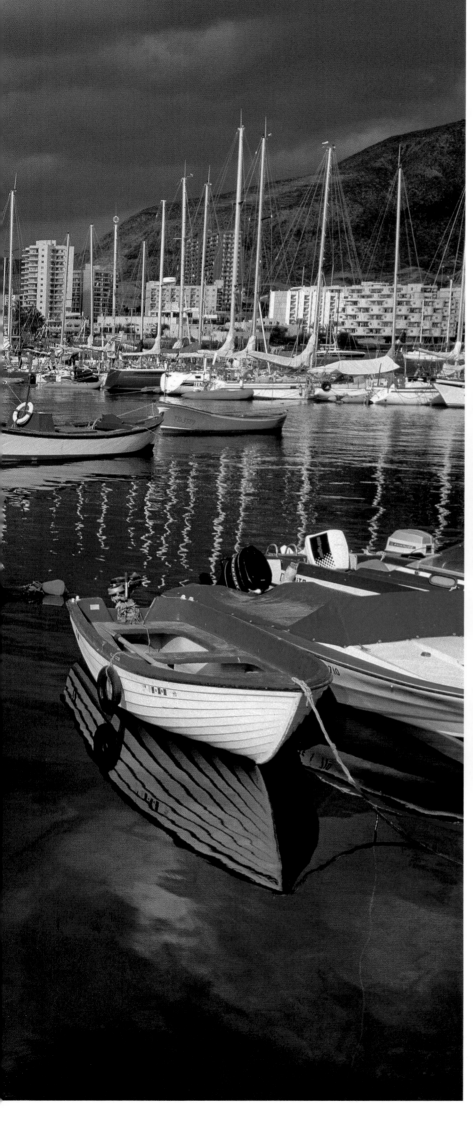

The Canary Islands

42-43 The best season for crossing the Atlantic Ocean is autumn, so this is when ports fill up with sailboats preparing to set sail.

43 top Named Las Afortunadas by historians of long ago, Pliny rechristened the islands Old Dog from the Latin, can aris, in reference to the dogs populating them.

43 bottom Christopher Columbus also waited at the The Canary Islands in the harbor at La Gomera for the right time, and also because the woman he loved lived there.

44-45 The wave astern lifts the boat, rolling beneath the hull, pushing it forward, reemerging in foam just a few yards in front of the prow.

44 bottom When the wind is strong, gusts full of vapor hit the crests of waves, the sky turns milky white, and life on board becomes uncomfortable.

45 center On calm days, the sea becomes one with the sky, and the sun and clouds create strange shapes on the water's surface as we wait for better sailing conditions.

45 bottom The Sula bassana or gannet is a large marine bird with a tapered body and narrow wings perfectly configured for diving into the sea.

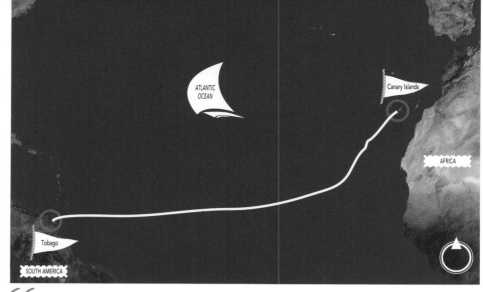

" *2,950 Miles. Three and a half weeks among the waves and endless sky without seeing land or even any other ships, just the trade wind, cirrus clouds, and the welcome company of dolphins and flying fish.* "

The Atlantic

THE FIRST CROSSING

The prospect of having to cross an ocean is a daunting one. The thought of conquering that enormous distance, the fact that we won't be able to stop if we need to, the awareness that we don't know how much time it will take, all these things contribute to creating an uneasiness around the difficult task ahead. The day of departure arrives, the land disappears in just a few hours and we suddenly find ourselves again in an alien world, in the midst of roaring waves and white spray. We feel awkward and bewildered in this volatile sea, experiencing a great sense of alarm. The pitching is constant and incessant, and the only place where we can relax is on our bunks, but even there we have to hold on. Every physical movement, even the easiest and simplest act of standing up requires sacrifice. It takes the force of a strong will to go out and check the sails, to decide to cook, to generally take stock of the situation, and just to go to the bathroom. The nights are long and dark and our shifts seem endless, immersed in a black sea without any glow from a coast or even the friendly light of another boat. So goes our first day, our second, and our third, if perhaps just a bit less intensely so. Then one morning we get up and realize that the rolling no longer bothers us. We look around and discover that the vast expanse of white-capped waves no longer scares us, in fact, it fascinates us and we watch while holding onto a stay, amazed at how a landscape made from nothing but water could be so beautiful.

After one week, our physical discomfort disappears while our psychological unease is diminished. Certainly, we still anxiously await the sight of land, but it is a distant nostalgia that no longer hurts. Meanwhile, our bodies learn how to coexist with the rolling sea. Our muscles learn to relax and follow the rocking motion of the boat. We discover we are capable of moving agilely while always holding onto something, naturally passing from holding on in bed to holding on while cooking, from holding on to the stair rail to holding on to the rudder handle with hands that instinctively guess where to grab, leg muscles that work autonomously to maintain the body's balance, while our hearts and spirits start to accept the idea of a home that is continuously moving within an empty horizontal plane at the center of an endless panorama.

Thus pass days and weeks, during which the empty sea that dismayed us becomes our friend and companion, so familiar that when the horizon breaks after so much time, allowing us a vision of the so longed-for low and misty landforms, of course we are pleased, but not as relieved as we first imagined.

46-47 During the longer stretches of sailing, dolphins are often our only company and there are sometimes up to 100 of them near our boat, staying for hours to play around the hull.

47 top and bottom Flying fish use their wing-shaped fins to glide briefly over the waves in an effort to escape predators below. At night on the high seas flying fish are carried aboard by waves and you can harvest them from the deck like windfalls.

47 center The old sextant is still a valuable tool for navigation, even when compared with more sophisticated and accurate electronic instruments.

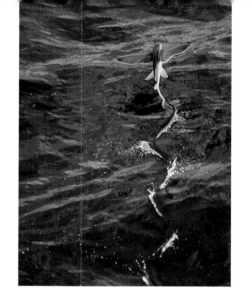

The Atlantic

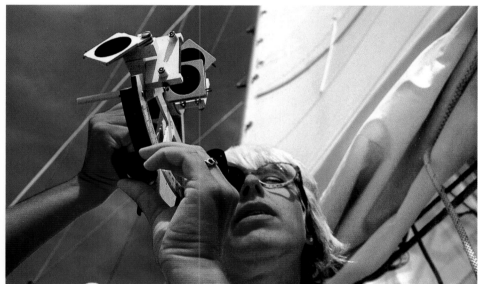

48-49 After 28 days of ocean, we now anxiously anticipate coral and shallows while maneuvering to get the wind to carry us to the place where we expect to anchor.

48 bottom Composed of two islands, the Republic of Trinidad and Tobago's capital is Port of Spain, on Trinidad. The republic gained its independence on 31 August, 1962.

49 With the boat's assistance, the net is positioned in the sea and subsequently hauled on land with the coordinated effort of many people.

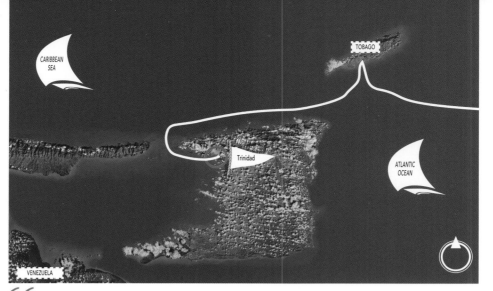

> At the other side of the ocean we find a new world full of fresh aromas, food, novel colors, and music. All of which dazes and confuses us.

Trinidad and Tobago
SO CLOSE YET SO DIVERSE

Our Atlantic crossing lasted 28 days, during which time our most recurring thought was of reaching the other side and sighting land. But when that morning came just after dawn and a dark spot materialized with the passing hours, as it became increasingly defined so we become progressively panicky. Tobago is here, just where we had expected to see it, but although everything seems to be going well, though the day is beautiful and the sun illuminates the island as it grows larger as we approach, nervousness crackles through the air on board. After so many weeks at sea in a world made of water, we have become enveloped in the security blanket of sailing towards a limitless horizon in front of our boat's prow. This limitless horizon allowed us to proceed undisturbed. All that concerned us was to check for tangling lines or changes in the wind, but coastlines or rocks to be avoided did not worry us – we had the freedom of the seas. Now, everything is different and we have to think about coral reefs and shallow depths, we have to maneuver and precisely position the sail to get the wind to carry us to a place where we anticipate dropping anchor.

Tobago becomes progressively more defined, we see the deep green-colored mountains now, the soft green plantations halfway up the coast, and the white buildings. Fresh produce is closer now – a steak, hot bread – and to be able to spend the whole night sleeping without having to wake up every three hours in shifts. All the things visualized in our daily waking dreams that now suddenly no longer interest us as much as they did. By now, we can see the port clearly, squeezed behind a small bay with black rocks on the left, rising out of the sea and climbing up the mountain, a beach in the center with palm trees and bushes, and threatening port

structures on the right. But, it doesn't matter because we are planning on anchoring in front of the beach. We lower the sails and turn on the engine, preparing to anchor, and begin to maneuver into the little bay while our misgivings mount. Where is the best place to land? There aren't any other sailboats and we do not see anyone around. What if it is an off-limits zone? The nautical chart doesn't say but things could have changed after it was published. What if something bad were to happen at night? If we aren't anchored well to the seabed, will we end up on the rocks? What if … . We change course, facing the sea, hoisting the sails, and start sailing again.

The next day, grey and rainy, we arrive at Trinidad, in the bay at the Port of Spain, a place that is decidedly less beautiful with an entry canal delimited by shipwrecks, in a dirty and dangerous city port. However, we will have 24 hours to adapt our minds and bodies to the idea of returning to dry land, which was, after all, our original intention.

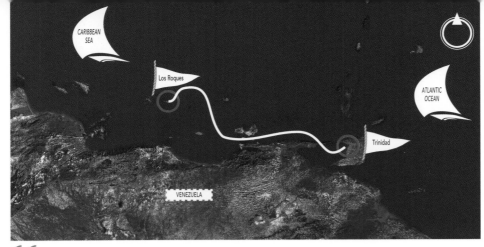

" 350 Miles. After four days along the Venezuelan coast we arrive at Loss Roques, entering a world of spectacular nature, color, and pelicans. "

Los Roques

CORAL REEFS AND PELICANS

As we gradually climb the path among the rocks, things are increasingly less hospitable, and the shrubs to which we cling become more fragile and sparse. There are no more palm trees or flowering plants, just stiff worn brush that resists the incessant trade winds. However, the view at the top is extraordinary. The Venezuelan coast with its bright and overcrowded cities is just a few dozen miles away, but appears to be remotely distant from this little island in the archipelago of Los Roques and we are surrounded by the blue of the boundless ocean.

We stay here for a week. It is a week spent losing ourselves among the stunning colors and shapes of the coral barrier reef and its inhabitants, or walking along miles of empty beaches. Pelicans surround the boat in the afternoon. They plunge into the sea and then reemerge with the soft sack beneath their beaks quivering with their catch of fish. They continue for hours, calling stridently, sighting fish, plunging in repeatedly and emerging victorious. They

retreat only when night starts to fall. We are anchored between the reef and a small island. There are no other sailboats but two launches with local fishermen pass by every morning. They are little more than boys, yet from the first day they stop to ask for a coffee, a glass of water, or to exchange a few words. We ask them how to make a line in order to fish in the bay, but given our poor results they stop every afternoon when they return, bringing us a fish, a lobster, or a basket of clams. In exchange, we give them fishing line, hooks, T-shirts as well as a couple of books and colored pencils. It is these young fishermen who gave us the directions to the hill we have just climbed. From up here, we can see the entire lagoon with the islands stretching out in the distance. The closer to the islands so the turquoise of the sea changes its intensity and progressively becomes lighter until it reaches a ring of white sand around the bright green stain of a flat island covered only by grass and palm trees, or the neutral green of a larger island with some low hills and denser vegetation. From up here, we become aware of the incredible number of pelicans that live in this archipelago. Focused on observing those that were fishing near the boat, we did not see the thousands of others that populate the remainder of the islands.

As we watch the pelicans, we notice something amiss. A red dot enters our line of vision. It looks like our rubber dinghy. We look further down at the water's edge to where we left it near the base of the hill. There is nothing there and that dot in the distance is really it, our dinghy, moving towards the ocean. If it leaves the bay, we won't be able to recover it and that would be a catastrophe! We run down the hill, jumping among sharp and stinging shrubs. We reach the beach skinned up and wounded, just in time to see our fishermen's launch appear towing our rubber dinghy. "Hombre, donde esta el ancla?" the boys laugh good-naturedly. Our oversized anchor remains in the sand of the seabed just a few steps away from us because the knot tying off the anchor came undone. We had prepared ourselves well for the ascent armed with cameras and tripods, but had forgotten to check the knot on the anchor line!

50 bottom Anchored in the middle of a blue sea is like being suspended, rising and falling, in the midst of nothingness.

50-51 The Venezuelan coast is just a few miles away but its lights seem very distant from this islet with only the blue of the boundless ocean around us.

51 bottom left Happiness is to exit the boat's cabin and find yourself in the cockpit inundated by the Caribbean sunlight as you admire the turquoise sea.

51 bottom right Coral reefs are rocky formations that constantly change due to the living polyps that shape them.

Los Roques

52 top Mountains of queen conch shells (Strombus gigas), a much appreciated mollusk in Venezuela, are the preferred spots for gaviotas (gulls) to lay their eggs.

52 center Gulls and terns frequent the islands of Los Roques by the millions, feeding on fish and small shellfish that they capture in the rich warm waters of the archipelago.

52 bottom In the afternoon, pelicans join us around the boat. Spying their fish prey below, they dive from great heights into the sea.

52-53 At low tide, the progressive retreat of the sea unveils a pristine strip of very white wet sand.

53 bottom With its toothed bill, the flamingo (Phoenicopterus rubber) filters out crustaceans suspended in the water that give its feathers the stereotypical pink color.

Los Roques

54-55 Both bright and pale-colored houses in the village on Gran Roque create a pleasant contrast with the gray rock that constitutes this island.

54 bottom left With a very white Spanish colonial style façade, the church at Gran Roque rises over the sand just a few yards from the sea.

54 bottom right Taking advantage of the tidal range, fishermen position their net, driving fish inside it.

55 To move from one island to the other, the only means of transport is the boat and fishermen are the only people authorized to spend the night on uninhabited islands here.

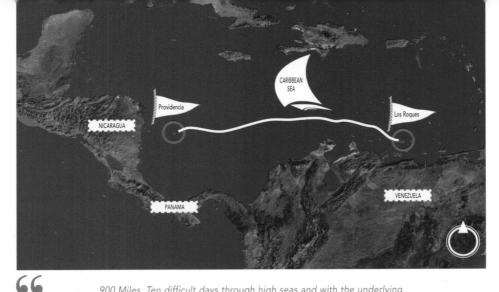

" *900 Miles. Ten difficult days through high seas and with the underlying threat of pirates to reach an islet inhabited by the descendants of a corsair.* "

Providencia

THE PIRATE ISLAND

On a map of the Caribbean, Providencia is little more than a dot. But according to legend the descendants of Morgan, the pirate who terrorized the Antilles and had his base at Providencia, still live on that dot today. Our crossing from Venezuela to Panama proved to be more tiring than we had expected because of strong winds and high seas, and also because we had chosen a route quite a ways out from the dangerous Colombian coast for safety reasons. Looking at the map, we realize that we can reach Providencia by traveling only 100 miles (160 km) further than initially planned. One hundred miles in exchange for a tranquil nest where we can wait for better weather. Unfortunately, except for that dot on the regional map, we have no other detailed map of Providencia. On the nautical chart we do find an in-depth description of the island

and its coasts, so we think why not try to design a map ourselves? While the wind and waves rage outside, we cling to the map and begin to draw.

We start by marking three black dots in the center of the paper, which are the three principal peaks described by the nautical chart, giving a very detailed description of their position. Then there is a point 2 miles (3 km) further north designating another peak, so we also draw that one, then a small inlet 3 miles (5 km) to the west of another peak so we add the creek. Gradually, and with not too much difficulty, we find that we have made an approximate sketch of the island with correct proportions. We mark the coral reef and the route to enter the lagoon, scattered rocks, anchorage, and island layout, everything in accurate alignment. Let's be honest, the first sailors arriving here did not even have this much! Inspired by the resolution of our daring predecessors and with a degree of reverential awe, we move closer to the reef, one of us taking the rudder and the other at the crosstrees in order to get a better view of our route from above. Due to the alignments indicated by the nautical chart, referencing one of the three peaks, we located an entrance to the lagoon. Then to find the little port of Santa Catalina we need to locate "Morgan's Head," a large rock whose silhouette naturally resembles the pirate's features. We look for it for more than a half hour, but our search is in vain. Perhaps we have been too optimistic and our makeshift map is not as accurate as we hoped. We decide to proceed, sailing by sight and checking the viability of our route from above. It is a real slalom course among blocks of greenish coral that luckily contrast perfectly with the very clear azure water. We pass by a boulder, avoid another one very quickly thereafter, and yet another. We move forward like this for an increasingly stressful hour and with every yard the little port opens up in front of us and with it "Morgan's Head" appears in all of its splendor. It is part of a rocky ridge on the western side that perfectly reproduces a human face with a forehead, nose, lips, and even bushes that recall curly hair. However, it is a shame that it is only visible when inside the bay.

56 bottom Crossing from Venezuela to Panama proves to be more tiring than expected, so with just a 100-mile (160-km) deviation we head for Providencia.

56-57 This large rocky formation, known as Morgan's Head for the pirate, perfectly reproduces a human face, welcoming whoever comes here to Providencia.

57 bottom left According to the season, fishermen move from one side of the island to the other to work, sheltered from high ocean waves.

57 bottom right The inhabitants of Providencia claim that they are descendants of Morgan, the pirate who terrorized Spanish colonies in the Caribbean during the 17th century.

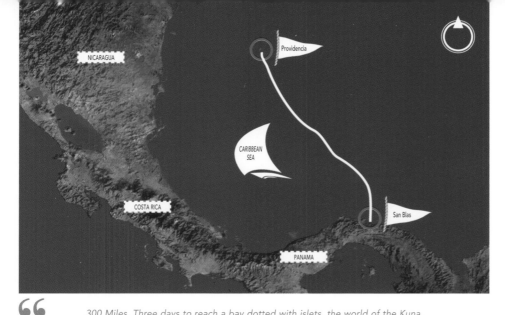

" *300 Miles. Three days to reach a bay dotted with islets, the world of the Kuna, an inimitable people who knew how to resist the arrival of the European explorers.* "

San Blas

INDOMITABLE INDIANS

The ritual ceremony celebrating a girl's puberty and her coming of age is one of the most important in the tradition of the Kuna and involves the entire community living throughout the islands of the Gulf of San Blas. With its canal crowded with ships, Panama is quite distant from this archipelago, which politically belongs to the country but enjoys total autonomy. The sheltered gulf hiding the islands has protected these people over the centuries from attacks by conquistadors and the coral reef has made sailing in the archipelago dangerous, while malaria exterminated those arriving by land, maintaining the indomitable independent spirit of the Kuna. Thus, a community of native peoples still lives today according to pre-Columbian customs in this hidden niche along the coast of Central America. Columbus was the first European to sight the San Blas Islands. He described them as plentiful as the days in the year, but not all inhabited. It is still that way today as inhabited islands only make up some of the more than 300 islands in the archipelago.

Others are covered by thousands of palm trees whose coconuts constitute the primary source of sustenance for the Kuna.

Shortly after our arrival we go before the *Cacique*, the chief of the community, and he gives us permission to stay here. It is he who invites us to the coming of age ceremony and celebration. It takes a few days for the Kuna to arrange everything, because the girl's family must prepare an enormous quantity of *chicha de cana*, which is a liquor made from fermenting cane sugar and fresh sugar. Once the day is determined, the girl and other female members of her family take their place beneath a canopy of palms. Around them, we witness the comings and goings of pitchers full of *chicha*, people bringing gifts and other beverages, while the female relatives bind the girl's wrists and ankles with bands of colored glass beads. These beaded bands will remain with her for life as her tribal ornaments and will prevent her, among other things, from fully developing leg and forearm musculature. Women taking turns giving her the liquor and advice have the same kind of ornaments, and their wrists and ankles look like those of little girls.

As the hours pass, the air becomes saturated with odors, the acidic scent of sweaty bodies, sweetness of pipe tobacco, and the alcoholic smell of the liquor that all drink in generous quantities. Some women start feeling poorly and are taken into the open air, but others cope by lying on the ground waiting for their turn at drinking. Despite the oppressive air, noise, and inebriated people, we are positive we have witnessed an important scene, something that has been repeated for centuries according to the same traditional ritual. On her wedding day, the girl will receive a ring in her nose, confirming her status as a Kuna woman. Like other women in her family, she will be a strong and capable of confronting a hard life on the islands. A woman who is proud of her origins, origins that she will always carry with her by wearing her traditional dress and ornaments proudly. She will be a woman that will raise her children according to the same dictates of pride and independence that will permit the Kuna people to continue, unscathed and intact, into the third millennium.

58 bottom *Panama seems much further away than the 80 miles (128 km) separating it from this archipelago, which officially is a part of Panama yet enjoys complete autonomy.*

58-59 *The hidden gulf, the insidious coral reef, malaria, and the aggressive spirit of the Kuna protected these islands from any assault by the conquistadors.*

59 bottom *An archipelago with as many islands as days in the year is how Columbus, the first European to sight them, defined the San Blas Islands.*

60-61 The Kuna live in huts constructed with palm fronds, each one a small pile dwelling with its own bathroom, linked to terra firma via a ramp with a passage beneath that acts as a natural drain directly into the sea.

61 top The traditional garb of Kuna women is the mola, a length of fabric formed by multi-colored layers with a design created by clipping into the various layers.

61 center Kuna women flaunt their traditional clothing and ornaments, proud of their origin and the indomitable spirit of their people.

61 bottom On reaching puberty, girls' wrists and ankles are adorned with colored glass bead bracelets and anklets that remain there for life.

San Blas

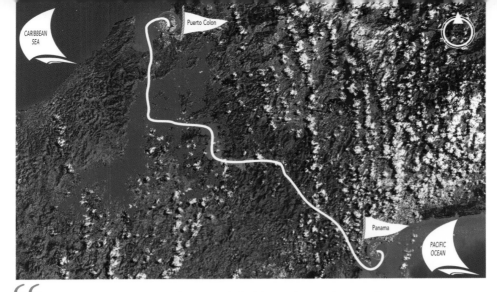

CARIBBEAN SEA

Puerto Colon

Panama

PACIFIC OCEAN

" *40 Miles. Two days across locks, lakes, and mountain cuts, sailing from west to the east, and we move from the Atlantic to the Pacific.* "

The Panama Canal

LINKING TWO OCEANS

If it were not for the Panama Canal, only the very courageous would be inclined to take a world tour in a sailboat. The Canal provides an easy journey of just 40 miles (64 km) from the Atlantic Ocean to the Pacific through the warm and calm waters of a canal and a lake, and a quite fantastic tropical environment. Without it, the alternative would be to sail down into the stormy southern latitudes and continue around Cape Horn. The Atlantic entrance to the canal is at the port of Colon, where everyone must sail to the first large lock. The gates that close behind us are as high as an eight-story building. Lines are thrown down from above to tie off the prow and stern, impeding the vortices that form when water is allowed to flow into the lock. The canal operators speak Spanish, we speak Italian, our assistants are French and American, the boat on the left is German, and the one on the right is Portuguese. In the midst of this Babel of voices calling out directions, questions, and curses, the water rises quickly, full of eddies and undertows.

There is a moment of calm when the water completely fills the lock, then the gates open and we find ourselves confronting an enormous ship with its prow towering above as it heads in the opposite direction. The ship's side runs past us on the right, sailors look at us from above and then it is suddenly time to enter the second lock and then the third. At the end, we have risen almost 90 feet (27 m) and enter Gatun Lake, which is an artificial lake created by the construction of the Gatun Dam and forms an integral part of the canal system. The lake water is green, its shores are covered with jungle, and old partially submerged skeletal trees mark our journey. At sunset, we drop anchor at the edge of this water highway, where boats of all sizes, shapes, and registries pass the night together. The next day we enter the Galliard Cut, a 7-mile (11-km) waterway that worms its way between two rocky cliff faces along the only part of the canal that was artificially excavated. The canal was cut through the mountain using the comparatively rudimentary means of construction available 100 years ago. An enormous cargo ship proceeds in the opposite direction and with one mistake on its rudder it could crush our boat against the mountain. After that bottleneck, we pass through the three final locks in rapid succession, bringing us further downward with each stage. Exiting the third and through a trick of topography we are now further to the east than when we left the Atlantic side, but now the waters of the Pacific Ocean are beneath our keel. There is still one mile of the canal to go, wide and easy. We pass under the Bridge of the Americas, which carries the Pan-American Highway, physically uniting once more the two continents which the canal had separated, and finally the Pacific Ocean opens in front of us. We have arrived! We leave the other boats with a farewell in all languages, hugs, and promises exchanged. We have conquered the Panama Canal together and now disperse, but we will soon see each other again in Tahiti, perhaps, or further along in our journeys, who knows where…

62 bottom To journey through the Panama Canal, sailboats are grouped in threes and there must be at least four people on each boat to operate the lines.

62-63 The Gullinard Cut is the only part of the Canal that was excavated 100 years ago, cutting through the mountain with the equipment available.

63 bottom left A two-day crossing through the warm waters of a canal and a lake, instead of months of sailing through the freezing storms of the southern latitudes.

63 bottom right It takes just a few minutes to refill the lock as the water enters rapidly, forming an impressive whirlpool, and rises very quickly to 30 ft (9 m).

64-65 The only land within 100 miles (160 km), this island is surrounded by a sea rich in fish, which includes a healthy population of sharks.

64 bottom This island was a good hideout because winds in the area were nasty and unpredictable, and clouds often shrouded any landforms.

65 bottom The Green Boat is seen here anchored inside one of the many grottos punctuating the island's coast – the destinations of treasure hunters.

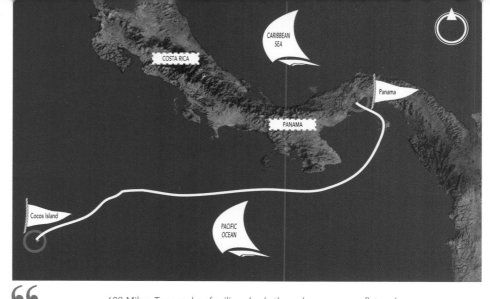

" *600 Miles. Two weeks of sailing slowly through an ocean as flat and peaceful as a sheet of ice to arrive at an enchanting island.* "

Cocos

TREASURE ISLAND

According to legend, pirates that attacked the Spanish galleons full of gold voyaging from Peru to Panama had a secret hideout on Cocos Island. The island was hundreds of miles away from any other land and a good hiding place because winds in the area were tricky and unpredictable. The winds would often calm for weeks, making any pursuit difficult and dangerous. Additionally, the island's cover of thick brush provided many places to hide and also its intricate labyrinth of caves were accessible only at particular times in the tide. It is said that in those caves the pirates hid their booty. The days of the pirate passed and later there came treasure hunters who arrived on the island, more or less secretly, to search for the hidden chests of pirate loot. Many of them spent years in total solitude excavating and probing for legendary hidden treasure on this deserted island.

A handful perhaps found some things, others died without success, and there were also a few who went crazy. And now it is our turn to arrive, also victim to the allure of Cocos Island. We were lucky to have been enveloped by a beautiful calm during our crossing. On certain mornings, the boat was completely immobile in the midst of a sea as smooth as a pane of glass. The hull was reflected in the water while the equatorial sun rose slowly and pitilessly. When the island finally appeared, it looked like a flower floating on the water. The green of its vegetation was so intense and unbroken that we could not even pinpoint the exact contours of the mountain that forms this solitary land.

We anchor in the deep waters of a bay. On land, the bed of a small stream leads uphill to a grassy clearing where the forest rangers live in their hut, the only inhabitants of what today is a Costa Rican natural park. The rest of the island is undisturbed forest, streams, and waterfalls that plunge into a sea full of coral and marine animals. A spectacular giant manta ray comes to dance in the shallow waters beneath our hull. We ascend a stream bed, write the name of our boat on the boulders in the bay as other sailors have done over the centuries, swim safely among the hammerhead sharks that patrol among the coral reefs, climb up the mountain to the grassy areas punctuating the higher jungle, and it no longer seems so impossible that a treasure could still be hidden here even after all these centuries, guarded only by the verdant and impenetrable vegetation on this isolated and breathtaking island.

Cocos

66 top Sailboat crews stopping at the island over the centuries carved their names on the boulders lining the beach here.

66 bottom left Today, Cocos Island is a Costa Rican natural park with no inhabitants, except for a group of park rangers.

66 bottom right The tangled underbrush on Cocos Island, full of roots and hiding places, is the ideal habitat for large land crabs.

67 A freezing-cold, roaring waterfall could be a good guardian for hidden treasure.

68-69 Accompanied by a park ranger, only local boats may sail among the Galapagos Islands and on land you must keep to the marked paths.

68 bottom In the cold waters of the Galapagos it is common to encounter schools of seals that will approach to within just a few yards of you.

69 center Sailboats must obtain a permit in advance, otherwise they are only allowed a 72-hour stopover for supplies.

69 bottom Puerto Ayora is the port of entry for all those arriving from Panama and you must leave your boat anchored here during excursions to other islands.

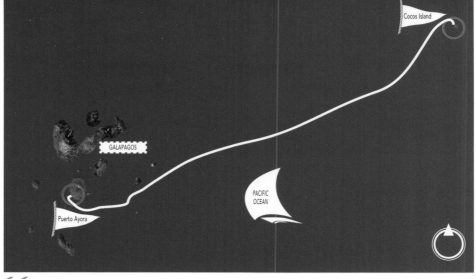

"

*450 Miles. Eight more days of calm seas and light winds to reach
the magical and unique world of the Enchanted Isles.*

"

Galapagos
NOAH'S ARK

Sailboats intending to stopover at the Galapagos Islands must have a special permit, which must be applied for in advance from the Ecuador Consulate. With this permit, you can stopover for several weeks at the discretion of the local authorities. Without it, you may only stop for 72 hours to purchase water and other supplies. We had made our request months but had never received a response. According to the rules, we have to head directly to the island of Santa Cruz in Puerto Ayora, the government's capital where we can find out if we may stopover. We cannot anticipate what the authorities will decide so we plan to stay on a route that takes us close to the small islands we encountered earlier, so close that we can at least get a glimpse of this legendary place.

It is quite a foggy dawn when we begin to skirt the little island of San Cristobal. Despite the humidity, the coastline is arid and rocky, the only visible vegetation is very tall cacti. After a few miles of this bare landscape, a bay suddenly opens up behind a promontory. It is small with calm blue waters and a little beach of light-colored sand, full of dark-colored rounded boulders. We slow down and move in nearer. The bay is certainly more pleasant to look at than the arid coastline, but there is nothing extraordinary about it until something unexpected happens. The boulders on the sand, as if commanded by a magic wand, suddenly animate, moving together towards the sea, enter the water, and swim in our direction. They weren't boulders after all. They are actually seal cubs! Once we are aware of them, the first cubs are already just beneath us swimming around the boat, swirling below the keel, doing somersaults, reemerging from the water with shiny muzzles and whiskers covered with foam. In Just a few minutes, we have a good dozen little seals all around the hull, fanning and beating their tails.

We lower the sails and began running from stern to prow so that we won't miss even one of their welcoming pirouettes. Fearing they will leave, we frantically search for something to feed them. We try canned anchovies! Then we think about all of the fish that they already have available in this uncontaminated sea and opt for small pieces of bread. However, they are not interested in food at all, they just want to play and we do not want to miss even one minute of this show. The activity continues for about an hour until we hear barking from the shore. It is the leader of the pack calling the baby seals back to order. Reluctantly, or so it seems, the cubs return to the beach, energetically shake off the water, and lazily crouch back down on the shore.

We hoist sails and head straight for Puerto Ayora, deciding to stopover as long as possible in these enchanting and entertaining islands.

70-71 The marine iguana lives only on the Galapagos Islands and to reach its optimal body temperature of 98.6° F (37° C), the lizard remains on the volcanic rock for hours, warming up in the sun.

71 top The land iguana is the second largest animal in the Galapagos, feeding on leaves and the fruit of gigantic cacti that are abundant on the arid coasts of these islands.

71 top center The albatross is a common bird in cold waters, ranging as far as the Galapagos, following the cold spur of the Humboldt Current.

Galapagos

71 bottom center In the mating season, the male frigate bird flaunts a red throat pouch that it inflates to attract the female's attention.

71 bottom On Puerto Ayora outside the Charles Darwin Research Station, dozens of pelicans fish at sunset.

72 top Giant sea turtles, which were once very numerous here, gave their name to the islands because of their shells look like saddles, or galapago, to the Spanish explorers.

72 bottom Boobies and gannets, like the other Galapagos animals, have not yet learned to fear humans who have not inhabited the islands for long.

Galapagos

72-73 Sea lions, the largest
aquatic species on the islands,
are not disturbed by human
presence but may become
aggressive during the breeding
season.

Galapagos

74 top and 74-75 You only have to dive down a few feet to become the object of attention and amusement for seals, which dart up and pirouette with the intention of playing and entertaining.

74 top center A red crab climbs onto a marine iguana to clean its rough-textured skin by devouring any parasites on the surface. The iguana doesn't constitute a threat to the crab as it only eats seaweed.

74 bottom center and bottom Feeding on seaweed on the ocean's floor, the marine iguana also ingests the water it requires, expelling excess salt through a gland above its nose.

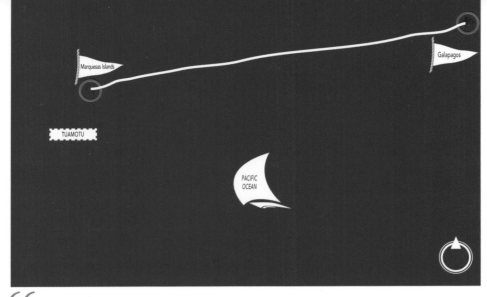

> *3,000 Miles. Three weeks of sailing with no breaks through the most extensive and empty ocean on the planet.*

The Pacific

THE PERSONALITY OF AN OCEAN

The Pacific Ocean is the largest, most desolate, and most mysterious of oceans. Certainly, we knew before encountering it that one third of the planet's surface is covered by water, but it is one thing to know it theoretically and another to find yourself for months in a watery universe made up only of waves, wind, and sky.

The Pacific Ocean crossing from the Galapagos to the Marquesas Islands involves a journey of 3,000 miles (4,800 km) and could take from three to four weeks. Twenty-two days of sailing in an absolutely empty ocean during which time we will neither encounter a ship nor a boat, and not even the trail of a plane in the sky. And finally, when we reach the Marquesas Islands, the great ocean will be far from conquered, we will only have completed one third of our route. It is true, from then on there will be no further huge, thousands-of-miles crossings because the trip will be punctuated by small islands that will allow us to break up the sailing and stopover at places with fantasy names such as Bora Bora, Tongatapu, Aitutaki, Suva, and Guadalcanal. However, these are very small pieces of land, grains of sand scattered randomly in an immense expanse of water, whose vastness is still a cause for anxiety, and only accurate and careful navigation will guarantee that these islands will appear in front of our prow.

When Magellan first crossed the Pacific during his circumnavigation of the globe, he did not encounter land at all. For three months, his ships crawled along from east to west as supplies diminished, fresh water became increasingly scarce, and the crews progressively discouraged along a route dictated by chance and by winds, probably just barely missing many islands without ever sighting one. Today, we have nautical maps and electronic instruments, and know in which direction to head, but those terribly small lands in their ocean universe – so enormous that Magellan never spotted one island – exist in an almost different world, a parallel dimension. Their remoteness and smallness have meant that their worlds have remained remarkably clean and pure.

76 bottom You sometimes won't have to touch the sails for days during a crossing, but once a storm develops, you must hurry to lower them.

76-77 When navigation becomes troublesome on the high seas, the best place to be is your berth because it's unlikely that any other boats may cross your path.

77 bottom One third of the planet's surface is covered by the waters of the Pacific, but it's one thing to know that, it's quite another to find yourself in that watery universe of nothing but waves, wind, and sky.

The Pacific

78-79 The dolphins love to come and swim near the boat as it sails, to play in the pressure surge that forms between the boat and the water.

79 top Dolphins swimming below the boat shriek imperceptibly, spreading their calls through the water until we hear it topside.

79 bottom After many days of sailing, our daily lives are made up of waves, sea, wind, sky, and sun, but also of lines and sails.

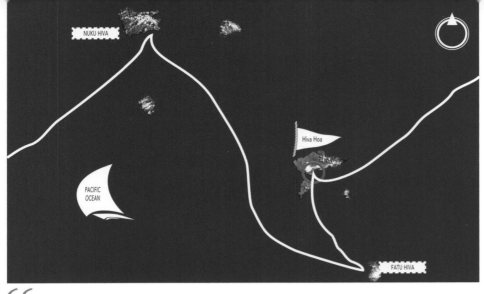

NUKU HIVA

Hiva Hoa

PACIFIC OCEAN

FATU HIVA

" At the end of our crossing we arrive at the Marquesas, 12 rugged and untamed volcanic islands where nature is the uncontested champion. "

The Marquesas Islands

MOUNTAINS IN THE SEA

After 3,000 miles (4,800 km) of Pacific Ocean, we arrive at the Marquesas Islands, high rugged mountains that look like gigantic stones thrown into the sea. These islands are the opposite of what you would expect from a tropical paradise as they are almost inaccessible with steep, plunging coasts perennially pounded by waves and deprived of any coral reef protecting them from the sea. The Marquesas have welcomed Melville, Stevenson, Conrad, Gauguin, Heyerdal, and so many other travelers who never became famous. All were attracted here by dreams, by the call of adventure, the fascination of discovery, and perhaps of finding paradise.

Many are the images that the Marquesas Islands offer to those who come from afar. The bay at Hiva Hoa with its black-sand beach, the village with coral houses, frangipani trees whose fragrance wafts through the air to anchored boats, and the corpulent and jovial women dressed in colored sarongs and flowers in their hair. The island of Fatu Hiva has a very narrow bay framed by stone pillars that took the name Baie des Verges (rods), but the missionaries wanted to change the name to Baie des Vierges (virgins). The girls make *tapa* fabric, that really isn't fabric, which is used to reproduce tribal icons and symbols related to their traditions. To fabricate this non-fabric, they beat tree bark for days on end and soften it in lime juice, incorporating colors made from ground berries and lampblack, and using brushes made from locks of their own thick black coarse hair. On Nuku Hiva, there are mountain gorges in the forest where waterfalls pour noisily into deep pools of water, producing great quantities of foam.

For us, the most vivid memory will be that of entering Atuona Bay after 22 days out in the Pacific, during which we had not even seen a plane or a boat. Just as we are dropping anchor, a boat comes out from the shore carrying someone to welcomes us with an enormous fresh grapefruit and a hot crunchy baguette. This is a veritable feast after weeks of crackers and canned food!

80 bottom The Baie des Verges (rods) on the island of Fatu Hiva. Missionaries wanted to rename it with the more innocuous Baie des Vierges (virgins).

80-81 High, rugged mountains that look like boulders thrown into the sea by a giant, these islands are the opposite of what you would expect in a tropical paradise.

81 bottom For sailors, the Marquesas present a difficult landing with rocky shores violently battered by waves and covered in impenetrable vegetation.

82-83 and 83 top Melville, Stevenson, Conrad, Gauguin, Heyerdal, and many others were attracted by the aura of adventure and mysterious secrets surrounding these islands.

83 center Beyond the forests, you enter a tangled world where vegetation of every size and variety competes to grow high enough to reach the sunlight each plant requires.

83 bottom H.M.S. Bounty, commanded by Captain Bligh, arrived in Polynesia to procure specimens of the bread tree, Artocarpus communis. A visit that resulted in some famous problems.

The Marquesas
Islands

84-85 Blue water here turns progressively lighter until it becomes an azure color over the impalpably luminous sand.

84 bottom After sailing, an open canopy over the cockpit is all you need to enjoy the peace and quiet of the atoll.

85 bottom The belts of coral enclosing the atoll are punctuated by motu, splendid little islands of coral sand covered with palm trees and low-lying vegetation.

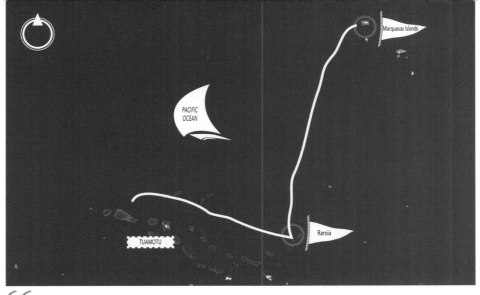

> *600 Miles. Six days at sea sailing from the raw nature of the Marquesas to the delicate tranquility of the Tuamotu Archipelago with endless beaches and turquoise lagoons.*

Tuamotu Archipelago

JUST ATOLLS

Raroia is our first bona fide inlet pass. It is a narrow corridor of blue water that suddenly becomes light in color and snakes through two outcropping banks of coral. It is a very light blue waterway between two brown strips through which our hull hesitantly advances. On the seabed beneath the keel, we pass over large rocks that the transparent water makes seem threateningly close. On either side, two high walls emerge intermittently from the sea. Following the directions from the nautical chart and the precise indications from the echo depth finder, we continue, hoping that the seabed in the inlet pass is sufficient for the not quite 6-ft (1.8-m) draft of our boat.

Our senses all seem to indicate that there is danger and not enough room: the sight of the forbidding, enormous rocks emerging from the water, the fearsome sound of the roaring current that pushes the water out of the narrow passage with the changing tide, and the smell from the algae and coral exposed by the escaping water.

Before tackling the passage through this channel, we waited outside the atoll for slack water between high and low tides, when the current in the inlet pass stops and then inverts. This strategy allowed us to proceed at a reduced speed in a light current that though it would impede our progress would also allow us to stop and turn around when faced with an unforeseen obstacle. When confronted with passages like this, we always climb the mast to reach the crosstree and so get a clearer view of our route from above. This is exactly what we did here, with one person at the rudder and another up the mast, remaining there for the few but interminable minutes required to cross that seemingly deadly threshold.

Then the world suddenly changes as the inlet pass widens, the current disappears, and we find ourselves in peaceful, quiet water, and we drop anchor on a seabed of very white sand. Outside, the trade wind continues to blow and the ocean to send its enormous waves crashing onto the coral reef. Inside, there is an unreal calm, a blinding light, and a lagoon full of an incredible amount of fish. Separating these two worlds is just a slim ring of barely emerged land, trimmed with white sand, covered with bright green bushes and a healthy population of coconut palms.

85

Tuamotu Archipelago

86-87 White sand covering the islands along the perimeter of the atolls is formed by madrepore particles from the erosion of the waves.

87 top Trade winds condense and form clouds over the atolls as they come into contact with the hot air rising from the lagoon waters, such that an atoll may be sighted from a distance.

87 center Beyond the coral reef, the trade wind continues to blow, but inside the lagoon there is a surreal calm, blinding light, and waters crowded with fish.

87 bottom Walking through the shallow waters of the lagoons, it is easy to bump into baby sharks swimming there because it is a "nursery" for them.

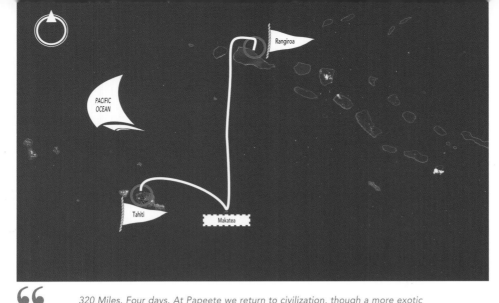

> 320 Miles. Four days. At Papeete we return to civilization, though a more exotic and relaxed one, scented with flowered tiaras and delightfully tempered by the natural rhythms of the Polynesians' way of life.

Society Islands

ESSENCE OF POLYNESIA

For us, French Polynesia begins with the mountains of the Marquesas and continues with the atolls of the Tuamotu Archipelago. However, there are also Tahiti, Papeete, Moorea, and Bora Bora. All magical, evocative names that inspire images of exotic and distant tropical lands, and which bring to mind the stories of Bouganville and La Perousse who told of green paradises with sweet fruit and fresh water after months of waves and scurvy. They made us think about the voyages of Cook who came to Tahiti

to observe the passage of Venus over the sun and christened the northernmost cape Point Venus, perhaps also in homage to the wonderful women of Papeete. They were liberal women who were happy, generous, and available, especially when compared with European women of that same period. Just a few years later they were the women who played a part in events that led to the mutiny on the H.M.S. Bounty, as it was the memory of their embraces that brought the mutinous sailors back to Papeete. Certainly, it was these women who fed the legend of the Society Islands over the past centuries, but who are now women who go to the office, stand in line at the supermarket, and take children to school on the backs of their mopeds. So what remains of that exotic world that made such an impression on the first Europeans? Much still remains, starting with the views of a spectacular landscape, the stuff of fantasies, and unique throughout the world. The deep green mountains of Moorea plunge into the two bays, giving form to the island. The pure and untainted water lagoon on Tahaa connects to Raiatea via reefs and white sand. The magnificent spectacle of the emerald-colored mountain at Bora Bora stretches into the deep lagoon of unbelievably transparent water. Then there are fragrances, such as the sweet and penetrating scent of the tiare, the symbolic flower of these islands, the intense flavor of vanilla fermenting in the sun, and the rancid odor of copra that ships pick up making their rounds of the islands and deposit on the docks of the port. Finally, there are the sounds, the music and songs that accompany every activity of these smiling and generous people. There are few places in the world that can boast of such a high concentration of beauty. Although Papeete is very much a modern city today, congested by traffic, filled with commercial activity, boats crowd its port practically stacked one on top of the other, and customs officials require crews in transit to pay a security deposit that they keep during your whole stay in the islands, and despite the cost of living being twice that in Europe, the Society Islands are still an essential stop for anyone making a world voyage. Even today it is not unusual for a crew member or two of a merchant ship to become bewitched by the enchanting beauty here and to decide to never leave.

88 center There is nothing more electrifying than being at the prow with binoculars, searching for any sign of land and better still if that land is a legendary one.

88 bottom The Society Islands, like the other archipelagos in French Polynesia, form a TOM, Territoire d'Outre-Mer (French outlying sea territory) with Papeete, on Tahiti, as its capital.

88-89 Cook's Bay on Moorea celebrates the great English navigator who, along with Wallis and Bouganville, made these Society Islands famous in Europe.

89 bottom Raiatea and Tahaa are enclosed by the same lagoon, surrounded by one coral reef, both having the same sort of light and scent of vanilla in the air.

90-91 Despite tourist development, the lagoon at Bora Bora is brilliantly maintained and is still as crystal clear as when it was described by the first navigators.

90 bottom Rugged mountains, soft, sloping hills, and green plains all resting beside a blue lagoon of warm water, overflowing with fish. These are the Society Islands.

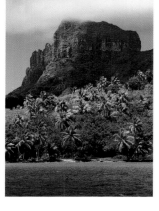

Society Islands

91 top The original name of the island in the Tahitian language was Pora Pora, meaning firstborn, which, according to local tradition, are the best and the most beautiful.

91 bottom Bora Bora is the icon of paradise in the South Seas, with its coral, blue and turquoise lagoons, white sand, palm trees, and mountains at its center.

92 bottom right Everything at Suvarov remains as was described by Tom Neal and the mariners that came to visit him during the 20 years that the hermit doctor remained on the island.

93 bottom Only the park ranger and his family, six people in all, now live on the island, making a minimal impact on the natural equilibrium of the atoll.

92-93 The Suvarov atoll, which belongs to the Cook Islands, has been declared a national park, with a museum dedicated to the New Zealand hermit, Tom Neal, who made it famous.

92 bottom left More than one boat has shipwrecked on the reef at Suvarov and crews were saved thanks to the provisions other visitors left in the care of Tom Neal.

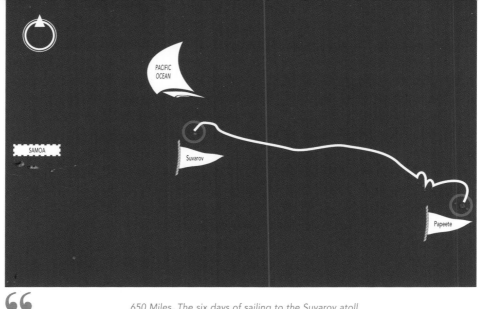

" *650 Miles. The six days of sailing to the Suvarov atoll is a refreshing break for the body and the soul.* "

Suvarov Atoll

TOM NEALS' GARDEN

Tom Neal was a New Zealand doctor who at a point in his life decided to become a hermit. He moved here to the uninhabited atoll of Suvarov, built a hut from Polynesian leaves and began to reorganize his life. He first dug a well in the coral sand in order to access the pocket of fresh water that exists beneath every atoll. He then grew diverse plants near the palm trees to guarantee his survival. In this way bread trees, papayas, and bananas appeared on Suvarov, and also a small plantation of sweet potatoes began to prosper. He started all this at the beginning of the 1950s when there weren't many boats passing by Suvarov. Tom welcomed everyone into his hut and asked that they behave according to this principle: *take what you need from here and leave whatever you have in excess.* Knowledge of his presence spread throughout the Pacific and during the 20 years he lived as a hermit visitors became more common, even including some famous ones who modified their journeys to search him out. A couple of boats were wrecked on the reefs at Suvarov and their crews were saved thanks to help from Neal and the supplies left behind by passing boats. Tom has now become a legend and the Cook Islands to which Suvarov belongs, have decreed the atoll a national park and museum dedicated to the New Zealand doctor.

We knew all about Tom Neal before we arrived, but Tanjijim, the old park ranger, repeats the story to us, one chapter after the other as he proudly shows us what remains of Neal's house, his still functioning well, the trees he planted that still bear fruit, and the wooden statue of Tom bearing a plaque engraved with his guiding principle. Tom Neal's choice was not haphazard: Suvarov is a unique place. An atoll lost in the middle of the ocean, populated by millions of

marine birds that go there to build nests, sit on their eggs, and care for their young until they are able to fly. It is a peaceful and protected place where the only predators are sharks that swim undisturbed even as close as the lagoon. Everything at Suvarov is still as Neal and visiting sailors once described it. Without that hermit doctor, who knows whether Suvarov would have been preserved as it still is today, free from aggressive Japanese and Korean fishermen, or phosphate miners.

The old park ranger shows everyone the remains of Neal's home and plantation, while instructing on how to move around the atoll. He explains where you may fish and where you may not, where you may collect coconuts and where you may not, where you may make a fire, and how to clean up after yourself on the beach. He also tells us that if we really need to, we can collect a few eggs. To find out if an egg is fresh, you just need to immerse it in water and, if it sinks, it is edible. However, we don't even dare try!

Suvarov Atoll

94-95 Millions of marine birds nest on Suvarov, sitting on their eggs and looking after their nestlings until they are able to fly.

95 top The coconut crab has disappeared throughout the inhabited islands because its meat is popular as it is rendered soft and sweet by the coconut on which it feeds.

95 center To guarantee a balanced diet, Neal cultivated bread trees, papayas, bananas, and a small plantation of sweet potatoes on the island.

95 bottom The park ranger and his family explain where we may fish, where we may collect coconuts, make a fire, and how to clean up after ourselves on the beach.

96-97 In the Western Samoa, inhabitants construct open houses, consisting of a roof supported by small wooden pillars over a platform.

96 bottom left The Western Samoa are made up of two larger volcanic islands, six smaller islands, and about 100 uninhabited islets.

96 bottom right Waterfalls plunge down along the old volcanic crater walls and water collects in hundreds of transparent freshwater pools.

97 bottom Deep blowholes in the coral reef siphon water from the waves, spraying columns of vapor hundreds of feet high.

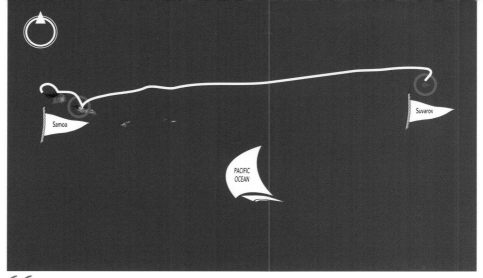

" *600 Miles. Six days of easy sailing pushed along by a consistent trade wind through the South Pacific to reach two volcanic islands with very few spots for anchorage.* "

Samoa Islands
OPEN HOUSES

Nature has been generous to the Samoa Islands, providing dense primary forests with intricate root systems and moss-covered trunks, flowers of every shape and size, springs that gush from the ground, bread, mango, and papaya trees that provide food and shade in all seasons. Survival here would never be a problem. Then, there are the natural phenomena such as the blow holes, deep natural wells in the coral reef that siphon off the waves and create columns of vaporized water dozens of yards high, waterfalls that plunge into the middle of lush green vegetation in old extinct craters, and lunar landscapes of lava fields studded with caves created by the rapid cooling of lava flows. It is a beautiful and seductive landscape where humans have thus far successfully adapted to living harmoniously with nature.

Apart from the rainy season, there is little that you have to protect yourself from on these islands. Thus, Samoans invented polygonal buildings to shelter themselves, constructed with a roof positioned over a platform, supported by small columns of wood and nothing else, no doors, no windows, no walls. As you pass these buildings you can see the few pieces that constitute furnishings: a table, a straw armchair, mats on the floor, and a few colored cushions. Walking among the houses after sunset, you can catch a glimpse of the inhabitants stretched out under mosquito nets sleeping or just chatting. The oldest houses are made of wood with palm-frond roofs, but some of the newer ones even have sheet metal and cement supports, but still conforming to the structure of the traditional dwellings.

Gaudy-colored buses provide transportation from one village to the other. The lower parts of the buses are metal, the upper parts are made from brightly painted wood. They struggle and rumble along the dusty roads, their vibrant colors contrasting with the lush green valleys. We take one of these sputtering buses to go visit the most well known of the island houses in

Apia, Villa Vailima, where Robert Louis Stevenson spent the last years of his life. There is nothing Samoan about the building, rather it is reminiscent of an English country residence with walls, doors, and oak floors imported from Scotland. In this restored home and part museum, you can perceive the love and respect that Stevenson still evokes today among the inhabitants of these islands. The writer only lived here for four years, but those few years were enough for everyone to accept him as a Samoan and revere him as a chief. Upon his death, the people of Vailima worked all night to cut a path through the woods to the top of Mount Vaea where *Tusitala*, their storyteller, had previously requested burial. In the morning, men took turns transporting his body along the path to the summit where his tomb still resides today.

A sensitive and enlightened man, Stevenson learned to see the value in local tradition and pleaded their cause to representatives of foreign governments who at that time were competing for possession of the islands. The difference between the destruction in the American Samoa and the dream-like peace of the Western Samoa is testament to his successful efforts.

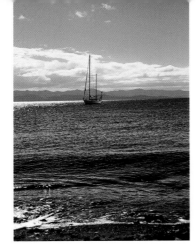

Samoa Islands

98 top Anchoring in the Samoa Islands, with the exception of the port at Apia, is difficult because of their deep waters and as a result they are always very private and secluded.

98 center A beautiful and seductive landscape where humans still live in harmony with nature.

98 bottom Western Samoa was the first country in the South Pacific to become independent in 1962, with Apia as its capital.

98-99 White coral beaches contrast with the black volcanic rock of the cliffs that occupy a great part of the islands.

100-101 A stark, white Catholic cathedral facing onto the port at Apia can be seen up to 20 miles (32 km) out at sea.

100 bottom Tusitala, "the storyteller," lived here for only four years, but those few years were sufficient to be accepted as a Samoan and revered as a chief by all.

101 top Maketi Fou is the central market at Apia and is open 24 hours, because vendors maintain night shifts so as to not lose their stalls.

101 center White buildings with red roofs, largely still maintaining their original wooden structures dating back to the colonial period, rise up along the sea at Apia.

Samoa Islands

101 bottom The wooden pastel-colored buses can take you to every corner of the Samoa Islands, struggling along through the wild vegetation on mountain roads.

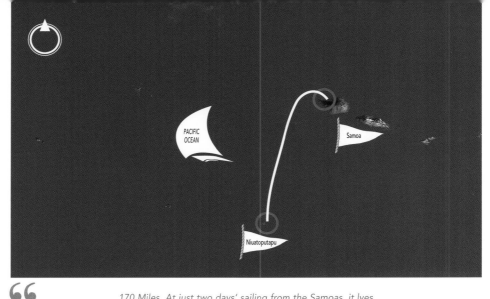

" *170 Miles. At just two days' sailing from the Samoas, it lyes the northernmost and most distant island of Tonga group.* "

Niuatoputapu

THE FACE OF DISTANT TONGA

"Welcome you who have come a long distance. For all of us, this lunch is a symbol of friendship that will endure over the years, even after you have returned to your own island." Our *island* is Italy where Rome is located and is very important because it is the same island where the pope lives! This was the first thing that inhabitants of Niuatoputapu wanted to know when, three days ago, we disembarked after conquering the convoluted inlet pass that feeds the lagoon and anchored near the village. They asked if we'd ever seen the pope's home, if we had ever been inside it, and if it was large. "Sunday, we'll prepare a welcome lunch for you and you can tell us about the pope's house!" And here we are, in the straw hut that, like all of the others in the village, is built over a carpet of grass. There are ornate *pandanus* (screw pine) mats with colored wool thread arranged on the ground. Seated on the mats, we witness a procession of children that enter, depositing bowls of food containing lobster, raw fish, roasted fish, slices of taro, seaweed dressed with lime juice, and papaya pudding. After we exchange greetings, there is a brief prayer of thanks then we begin to eat. Only we eat because our host family and all of the other Tongans present watch us, interrupting only to urge us to try this or that dish, to have some more, or to finish what remains in the bowls. They will eat what is left over, if we leave anything, and only when we have finished. It is like this on all of the islands in Polynesia. In the beginning when we did not know how things were, we made an effort to eat as much as possible, thinking it was rude to leave food. However, by observing the relief on children's faces every time we refused something, we learned that it is better to leave as much as possible. While we eat, we respond to their questions about the pope's home. Is it large? Yes, but many other people live with him. Have we been there? Yes, but not in the room where he sleeps. Yes, we have seen him, but no we have not ever touched him. Dozens of wide eyes watch us as the Tongans hang on our every word.

Niuatoputapu is the northernmost island in Tonga, away from tourist routes and in a splendid isolation. Years ago, someone attempted to develop a resort here, but failure of the airline connecting the island to the capital prevented potential visitors from reaching it. There is also a small ice factory regulated by the Japanese government that does an interesting demonstration not far from the beach, but no currency is in circulation on the island and we are their only customers. The lifestyle in this tranquil village continues its serene existence according to the rhythms of the sun and moon, as the people cultivate their small plantations of bananas, taro, cassava, and harvest the bounty of the lagoon.

104-105 Preparing the pandanus (screw pine) used to weave the kiekie, the traditional Tongan woman's skirt, is the most important activity on the island.

105 top Processing the pandanus requires weeks of work and the commitment of all the family members.

To be used in traditional items of clothing, pandanus must be bleached, remaining in sea water for seven days and seven nights.

105 center Life on Niuatoputapu is regulated by the rhythm of the tide and low tide leaves the reef exposed, allowing the people to process pandanus in a water bath.

105 bottom Niutoputapu was once linked to its capital, Nukualofa, by an internal flight but the airline's bankruptcy made the island even more remote.

Niuatoputapu

106-107 The Atolls of the Phoenix are in the same time zone as the Samoa Islands but maintain the same date as their capital, Tarawa, located on the other side of the International Date Line.

106 bottom The only means of transport to the Atolls of the Phoenix is by classic sailboat without use of an engine.

107 bottom The giant manta ray lives in the warm waters of the atolls and rarely goes off the coast where, even though it belongs to the same family as sharks, it feeds only on plankton.

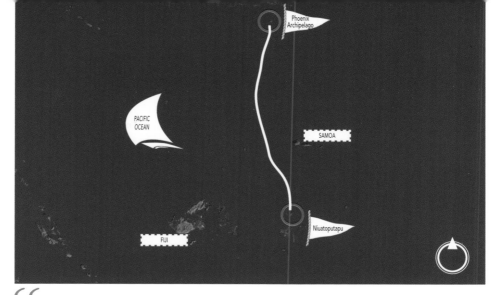

" *800 Miles. Ten days of tiring sailing, sometimes with a headwind, but with the rewarding objective of reaching a unique and exceptional place.* "

The Atolls of the Phoenix

A RICH SUPPLY OF BIODIVERSITY

To enter the inlet pass at Canton Island, you must wait for slack water when the tide changes and the current disappears for a minute. However, when it is the right time according to our charts, there is still a stream of water whirlpooling between the coral walls of the pass. We have to wait in open water, approaching slowly, to determine the opportune moment and, after just five hours, we successfully enter the lagoon! There must be a flaw in our calculations and after a few days we discover that Canton Island is in the same time zone as the Samoa Islands, but maintains the same date as its own capital, Tarawa, which is located 500 miles (800 km) further west, on the other side of the international dateline. We consulted the tide tables for the wrong day!

The Atolls of the Phoenix have always been uninhabited. No one, not even Polynesians, have ever been interested in these distant lowlands, devoid of water and trees, inhabited only by crabs and birds. In the first decades of the 1900s, however, the U.S. decided to utilize Canton Island, one of the largest atolls, as a landing strip for the first transoceanic planes that didn't have the flight range to cross the whole Pacific Ocean. They constructed a runway, a hangar, a hotel for passengers, a fuel storage depot, and living quarters for personnel with all necessary facilities, even including a natural swimming pool and basketball court. Then during the war, the airport became one of many from which aircraft departed to bomb the Japanese in the Pacific and the island was equipped with concrete bunkers camouflaged among the bushes. Once the war was over, the Canton Island airport was no longer useful and the Americans left, abandoning what they had built to the wind and vegetation. Only a small outpost of ten families sent by the Kiribati government now live on Canton Island. They live in the airbase ruins and are the only human beings within a radius of about one hundred miles. The rest of the island is completely

uninhabited. Wandering among the brush, you will come across old vehicles with hoods invaded by greenery, while in the groves of casuarinas you may suddenly come upon enormous tanks held together only by rust, with coconut palms growing between their twisted frames. It will still take a lot of time before nature finally smothers the havoc wrought by humans.

Other islands in the Phoenix archipelago, however, have never been touched. They remain unpolluted and wild – true paradises for birds and myriad kinds of marine life in the coral reefs. They are a unique treasure of the Pacific, a natural heritage to be preserved intact for the future. In 2006, the Kiribati government decreed the entire archipelago a marine park, the largest in deep waters in the world, turning down the money that Korea and Japan were willing to pay for permission to fish in these waters. This is a step of major importance on the part of a small country whose enormous moral strength safeguards an integral piece of our planet's ecology for future generations.

The Atolls of the Phoenix

108 top and center The channels around the Atolls of Phoenix are too shallow to allow a boat's passage into the lagoon, so you must anchor outside.

108 bottom and 108-109 Before becoming an adult, the awkward young bird flaps its wings but does not yet know how to fly and still only has tufts of feathers under its outer plumage. By approaching carefully, you may get within just a few steps of female boobies, and young birds may never have even seen a human being.

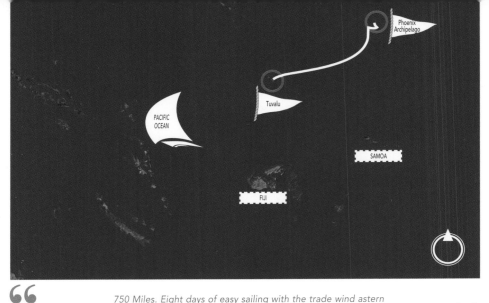

*750 Miles. Eight days of easy sailing with the trade wind astern
in these latitudes near the equator that treat us so well.*

Tuvalu

A SUBMERGING PARADISE

In only two of the nine islands that constitute the minuscule country of Tuvalu are there suitable anchorages for sailboats. So, after wandering around these spots, we leave the boat in the care of two Funafuti policemen and embark on the government ship that tours the most distant islands and which leaves from the capital every two weeks. We go on board along with drums of diesel, crates of chickens, pigs slung up in nets, rotund women, babies, children of all ages, and entire families who, with *pandanus* mats, cushions, and excessive amounts of food, are prepared to spend days and nights of the voyage on deck. We reserved the only cabin available, not so much for the worn out bed and dilapidated bathroom as to have an electrical outlet available to recharge the batteries in the video cameras.

There is an outlet in the room but the door does not shut securely, while the only window has no glass and looks onto the deck. In the few hours that we spend in the cabin, there is always someone looking into the window to offer us something to eat, a coconut to drink, or just to chat. Every two days we land at an island and at every new island we venture down the warped steps that lead to the launch where we crowd in with the locals, their goods and children – handed from adult to adult into the boat. Upon arrival we all pile out on to land with a great joyful noise of splashing, shouting, and laughter. Each stopover is a blast into the past where people have chosen to remain in villages, leading a naturally rhythmic and peaceful existence similar to that of their grandparents and great-grandparents. Today, however, a serious threat hangs over the serenity of these people. The effects of global warming and rising sea levels are seriously beginning to compromise life in this world. The Tuvalu Islands, just a few dozen inches above sea level, could become completely submerged in water over the course of just a few decades. Today during spring tides, the lowest-lying islands are already completely flooded with sea water, making the already scarce amount of available soil uncultivable. The United Nations has created the new status of *environmental refugees* for the inhabitants of these atolls, and some countries in the Pacific are already preparing to welcome those who will have to leave their homelands to escape the encroaching sea. The attitudes of the inhabitants varies from the disappointment and irritation of the young people, who blame industrialized nations for not respecting the Kyoto Protocol, to the calm resignation of older citizens, convinced that if God created the Tuvalu Islands He will also preserve them so that its inhabitants may continue to live here the rest of their lives.

110 bottom Along with the atoll that is home to the capital, Funafuti, the atoll of Nukufetau is the only one here to have a waterway capable of allowing entry into its lagoon.

111 Barely above sea level, Tuvalu will be one of the first archipelagos to disappear due to the effects of global warming.

Tuvalu

112 top Toddy is a liquid rich in vitamins and minerals and comes from the coconut palm. It supplements any deficiency of fruits and vegetables that are not produced on the islands.

112 center Thanks to the United Nations the people of Tuvalu are already categorized as Environmental Refugees in anticipation of the probable disappearance of these islands.

112 bottom This piglet is very
overweight because it is fed with
coconut cooked whole in the
traditional subterranean oven.
A food normally eaten by
islanders only during holidays.

112-113 The diet of the
inhabitants of Tuvalu is mainly
fish, usually tuna, which forms
a part of most of the meals and
often eaten raw.

114-115 Throughout the 25-mile (40-km) perimeter of the atoll, there is just one small portion of dry land, with a core of jungle bordered by a narrow thread of white sand.

114 bottom left During the dry season, many marine bird species stopover at Quelelevu to lay eggs right among the coral rock formations.

114 bottom right The only inhabitant of Quelelevu told us: "I was born here and here is where I want to die, this is my homeland. If my brothers, sons, and nephews want to see me then they have to come here."

115 bottom The bure is the Fijian traditional dwelling, constructed of wood and coconut palm fronds, arranged in such a way as to divert rain from seeping in during heavy storms.

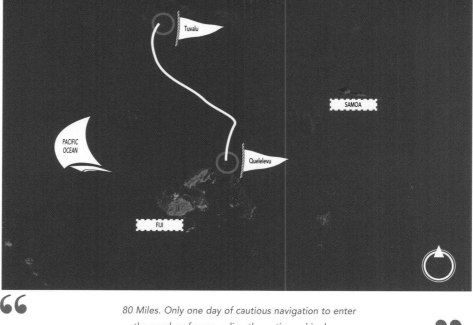
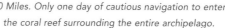

> *80 Miles. Only one day of cautious navigation to enter the coral reef surrounding the entire archipelago.*

Quelelevu

AN ATOLL AND ITS ONLY INHABITANT

When we disembark on the strip of sand at the eastern end of Quelelevu, there is only a dog to welcome us. He hops around us to celebrate our arrival then sets off as if urging us to follow him. Some 700 feet (200 m) further along is a clearing and behind some wooden planks covered with palm fronds sits Tico, the dog's owner and the only human being on the entire atoll.

Quelelevu is a ring of coral with a 25-mile (40-km) diameter. Ocean waves break on the outer rim of the reef, leaving the inner lagoon in peace and where enormous coral boulders give refuge to multitudes of marine birds. Only one small portion of the coral ring breaks the surface and on it is a clump of jungle bordered by a white sand beach – this is Tico's kingdom. Eighty miles (130 km) from the nearest island, Quelelevu is one of the most beautiful places that we have ever visited. The lagoon ripples with surreal colors, there are millions of birds, crabs, lobsters, water snakes, and many other creatures all living here undisturbed. Tico was born here 65 years ago when about a dozen people lived on the island. Like all coral islands, Quelelevu lies over an envelope of fresh water created by rain filtering through the coral. A small plot of land was cultivated, producing bananas, papayas, some tubers, and the usual coconut palms. The sea was rich with every God-given gift. The population then increased and the cultivable terrain was no longer sufficient to produce enough food, and even the freshwater stratum became overly depleted, turning to salt water. The people then moved to the main islands where there were more resources, they could work, and their children could go to school.

At 20 years of age, Tico found himself working in the capital as a security guard for a public building, then he married, had four sons, and now also has many nephews. Five years later, he decided to return here to Quelelevu. A fishing boat brought him back and he has not moved from this atoll since. "I was born here and here is where I want to die. This is my homeland. My brothers, my sons, and my nephews must come here if they want to see me." In the meantime, he shows us his kingdom, the *bure* where he lives, the space in the grove of trees where he's planted sweet potatoes and where the old papaya and banana trees have begun to prosper again, and the henhouse where he looks after the chicks born from hens that are almost wild now. "I don't want for anything here, I have work to do, and food to eat. Today, I worked in the garden all day then sat down and asked myself, where is my payback, and here you are."

116-117 Northeast of the Fijian islands, this large solitary atoll offers us some of the most beautiful, purest, and cleanest seascapes throughout the Pacific Ocean.

116 bottom Coconut palms need very little water and substrate to grow, develop, and produce dozens of coconuts full of refreshing fizzy liquid.

Quelelevu

117 top The giant clam, once widespread throughout the Indo-Pacific coral reefs, is now on the way to extinction due to its indiscriminate and unsustainable exploitation.

117 center Ocean waves break at the reef's exterior and do not disturb the peace of the inner lagoon.

117 bottom There is ocean all around us and the nearest land is 80 miles (128 km) away, yet the unexpected calm of this huge "saltwater lake" conveys the warmth of home.

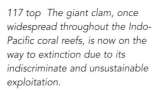

" *200 Miles. Four days of varied and complex navigation on a sinuous route among the islands and reefs of the Fijian archipelago.* "

Taveuni

THE ISLAND OF THE DAY BEFORE

The island of Taveuni is cut in half by the 180° longtitude, which is the meridian furthest from the Greenwich or Prime Meridian and marks the International Date Line. The village of Waiyevo, just west of the date line, is the first place in the world where the sun rises each morning. And at the same time each day the west side is 24 hours ahead of the east side. When it is Monday at noon on the west side, it is noon on Sunday on the east side. The Fijians are proud of this fact. It is the only country in the world that can boast of an island where this is possible because the only other land the 180° meridian intersects is in the polar regions.

On Taveuni, a large placard marks the passage of the famous meridian, but the first time that we see it, it clearly seems in error. On the east side is printed the word, "yesterday," while "tomorrow" is on the west side. "This is wrong," we say to the village chief. "That's true," he responds, "someone should change it to *tomorrow* on the east side and *yesterday* on the west side!" "No, *yesterday* is okay on the east side, but *today* should be on the west side." "*Today*?! No, that's not possible!" The chief does not exactly agree with us. Maybe the term "today" to him seems like something too magical relative to that invisible line that, according to him, must only have something to do with the past or the future. In the end after many discussions, even our certainty begins to falter. On the other hand, this imaginary line has always confused everyone, starting with poor Antonio Pigafetta who, despite shipwrecks, scurvy, battles, and storms, found the time every day to diligently document the first circumnavigation of the globe in his diary, the account of Magellan's unfortunate voyage. And how surprised and disappointed they must have been when, returning to Spain, they realized that they were missing one day! However, he was certain that he'd accounted for each and every day!

It would take some years for the most educated minds to arrive at an explanation. When going around the globe, you must subtract one hour for every 15 degrees of longitude traveled, and once you have circled the globe and subtracted one hour 24 times, you must add one day to agree with your fellow citizens who have never left their homes. The International Date Line has continued to impassion and fascinate travelers and writers over the centuries. Umberto Eco even wrote about it at length in *The Island of the Day Before*, inspiring tourists to dream about a journey into the past, flying from Fiji to California, leaving Wednesday evening and after an all-night trip, arriving at their destination on Wednesday morning!

118 bottom Currents forming in the channel between Taveuni and Vanualevu encourage the passage of schools of dolphins and whales.

118-119 A fantastic landscape left exposed by the tide along the more than 60 miles (96 km) of Taveuni's coastline, which is largely uninhabited.

119 bottom left The most beautiful seabeds and banks of coral throughout the Fijian archipelago are near Taveuni, one of which is Rainbow Reef.

119 bottom right The International Date Line is the first place in the world where, by convention, the sun rises and the west side is 24 hours ahead of the east side.

120-121 The high mountain at the center of the island causes clouds to condense, resulting in frequent precipitation and so there is rich vegetation here.

121 top Water abounds on this island where it rains almost every day, waterfalls form pools and small lakes, and at times, rush directly into the sea.

121 top center The sun's rays have difficulty penetrating the humid and tangled jungle, and only during the hottest hours of the day does light reach the lowest plants in the undergrowth.

Taveuni

121 bottom center The bilibili (raft), built with giant bamboo stalks and pushed forward with a pole, is the primary means of transporting people and goods along the coast.

121 bottom Immersed in the water, the women advance in unison as they focus on and harvest small fish that come upstream at high tide.

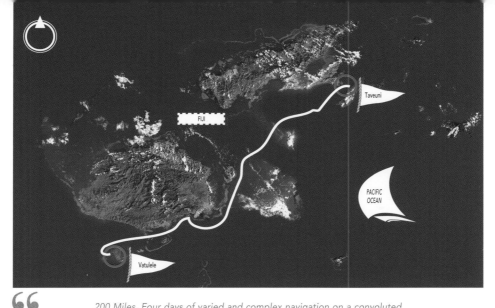

200 Miles. Four days of varied and complex navigation on a convoluted
route among the islands and reefs of the Fijian archipelago.

Vatulele

THE KAVA CEREMONY

It is hot in the hut but no one seems to mind. Everyone watches the old chief as he grasps the bundle of roots lying at his feet, raises it, turns it around in his hands, and begins a solemn chant. It is an ancient dirge with tones that rise and descend, directed both at everyone and at no one. It is a ceremony that has been repeated in the same way for centuries and that was once important to diminishing, if not eliminating, the risk of being killed by the savage warriors in these islands. The chief speaks and though we do not understand the words we get the gist of them: "These people have arrived from a distant island called Italy. Their names are Lizzi and Carlo. They have come to our island to see who we are and what we do. They have drunk the *yaqona*, our traditional drink, as a sign of friendship. Should we accept them into our village?" The ritual question is addressed to all those present in the bure. "*Yandina, Yandina.*" "Yes, we accept them" is their response. Other words are exchanged and then the chief smiles and for the first time addresses us in English: "You may stay here, you may visit our village, you may drink our water, collect our coconuts, and catch our fish." These simple words permit us to move around the island, to nose around the huts, to participate in village ceremonies, and become friends with everyone here. Until about 100 years ago, Fijian warriors were the fiercest and cruelest in the Pacific. Every island was at war with the next island, every village with its neighboring village, every man, woman, and child that found themselves defenseless in the forest was captured and beaten to death to then be eaten by victorious natives in a collective celebration. The few white people who have came to these islands during this time had horrifying tales of a world governed by unspeakable violence. Missionaries arriving later were armed only with words of justice and fraternity, bringing with them the rules of a strange religion from a distant land. Dozens of missionaries were mocked and eaten, but new ones kept coming, increasingly more stubborn, perhaps naive, and certainly indomitable. In the end, the

missionaries' words found their way into the hearts of the Fijians and they converted. It was a complete conversion without hesitation or reticence. In the last century, Fijians embraced Christianity with the same joyous ingenuousness they first devoted to tribal battles and grand cannibalistic banquets. They became hospitable, mild-tempered, and kind. Only the kava ceremony remains to recall that long ago period when all of them were warriors, when the whole world outside their villages was hostile and dangerous. The old man puts the powder from the bunch of roots into a watery infusion, producing a brownish liquid. Each one of us takes his or her turn receiving a bowlful, which must be drunk in one swallow. We follow suit with the Fijians present, clapping our hands three times as the others do, nevertheless trying not to turn up our noses at the muddy taste of this profoundly important ceremonial drink.

122 Until 100 years ago, Fijian warriors were savage and cruel, every island was at war with the next one, and arriving by sea could be risky for anyone.

123 bottom The Fijian islands have been independent since 1970 and are made up of three major islands, with another 300 minor islands and islets that are in large part uninhabited.

Vatulele

124 top The traditional kava ceremony remains to recall that long ago period when all the men were warriors and when the whole world outside of each village was hostile and dangerous.

124 bottom left The traditional bure huts can still be found in many villages, constructed over the grass, surrounded by flowers and frangipani trees.

124 bottom right The kava, root of the Piper metisticum, is sold at the market in a cone form characterizing the sevu sevu, a gift. It is then transformed into yaqona, a drink.

125 On special occasions, tubers and meat are cooked in the traditional lovo oven, then the food is served on napkins made from banana leaves.

126-127 Port Resolution, the only anchorage at the island of Tanna, owes its name to James Cook's ship, the first European vessel to enter this natural port.

126 bottom Vegetation throughout the island's perimeter is covered by a fine veil of black dust, a product of Yasur's constant eruptions.

127 bottom The anchorage at Tanna Island's capital of Lenakel is not sheltered so you must anchor among the waves, and when the wind blows southward disembarkation can be dangerous.

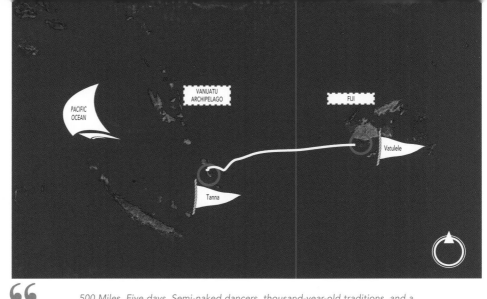

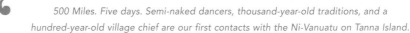

> *500 Miles. Five days. Semi-naked dancers, thousand-year-old traditions, and a hundred-year-old village chief are our first contacts with the Ni-Vanuatu on Tanna Island.*

Tanna

THE LAST TRIBE

Naked children run up to us. They take us to the men who are expecting us, also nude and seated at the foot of an enormous banyan tree. We are in the village of Yakel, the only one on the island of Tanna where the old customs are still followed. The body of traditions and rules that were compulsory for the Vanuatu before the arrival of white men. The Yakel people have the elders in the village instruct their children, cure themselves using only traditional medicinal herbs, consume only food that they can procure themselves, and only wear garments made from straw – long ankle-length skirts for the women and the *namba* for the men, which is a banana leaf worn around the waist that leaves their muscular bodies completely exposed. When the younger children sight an off-road vehicle in the distance bringing foreigners, they sound the alarm and the whole village mobilizes. Visitors thus find men, women, and children waiting for them in a clearing outside their village, welcoming them with song, jumping and stamping their feet in rhythm to an ancient chant. Once the Yakel people finish their dance, they pose for photos, sell some odd artisan items, and collect their fee for the visit. Tourists then leave after an encounter of not more than a half hour between two very distant and diverse worlds. However, we stay. We want to know whether we are really witnessing a tradition, left untouched by massacres and missionaries, or if it is just all a big act. We enter the village, walk among the huts, speak with women, young people, and play with the children. We return the next day and yet again the day after that. We witness the arrival of other tourists, other dances, and discover that reality is somewhere in the middle. There are men and women living in the villages around Yakel who, at the children's call, rush to dress in traditional garb of long ago and play their parts as savage natives. However, there is also a small group that still faithfully follows the ancient island customs in all aspects of everyday life. Their chief is named Kawia and says he is 102 years old. He is an old stooped and wrinkled man. His skin is like soft parchment barely covering his bones, and an old pipe and knife are slipped into the straw chord around his waist supporting the *namba*. With the aid of a young man who interprets his dialect, he

recounts the history of the tribe and his determination to defend the people of Yakel from the new thinking and lifestyle proposed by the white people. When we are ready to leave, the old man guides us to the *nakamal*, the space for sacred ceremonies where we have not yet been and we find all of the males assembled there, from the smallest children to the oldest, whose age can only be guessed at. They begin to sing and to move in unison, performing a dance that we have never seen before. They mime scenes from daily life, hunting expeditions, and duels between warriors. A light, freezing, and nagging rain falls from the dark and cloudy sky but the wet glistening dancers do not pause in a rhythm that steadily increases to a new level of intensity, drumming their feet on the muddy ground with a force that resounds in the earth beneath our feet.

Tanna

128-129 At Tanna Island gods and nature are celebrated with festivals and ceremonies, during which islanders paint their bodies and faces with natural pigments. During the toka, all of the clans on the island unite to dance and sing in a tribal festival in order to eliminate all resentment and grudges between them. Participants in the toka live outside in the open for three days and three nights, consuming food and water brought from home and sleeping just a few hours each night.

128 Yakel's village chief has imposed compliance to their traditional set of standards. Customs that were in force among the Vanuatu long before the arrival of white people.

PACIFIC OCEAN

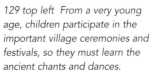

129 top left From a very young age, children participate in the important village ceremonies and festivals, so they must learn the ancient chants and dances.

129 top right According to custom, a Yakel warrior's headdress must be worn every day and may not be touched by a woman.

129 bottom Women fabricate their skirts with banana leaves that are first dried in the sun then cut to size once they are put on.

129

130-131 The volcano on
Ambrym does not erupt with fiery
material like the one on Tanna
Island, but the islanders say that
its dust may still influence their
crops.

130 bottom The Dugong dugon
is a mammal of the Sirenia order
that may reach almost 10 ft (3 m)
in length and half a ton in weight.

131 bottom The only anchorage
at Ambrym is on an open and
solitary bay on the leeward side
of the island, and the trade wind
reinforces the wind descending
from the mountains here with
very violent gusts of wind.

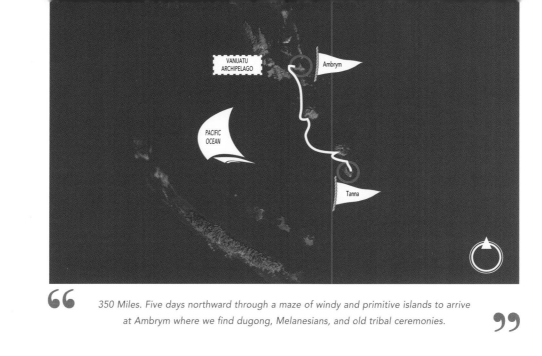

VANUATU ARCHIPELAGO

Ambrym

PACIFIC OCEAN

Tanna

" 350 Miles. Five days northward through a maze of windy and primitive islands to arrive at Ambrym where we find dugong, Melanesians, and old tribal ceremonies. "

Ambrym
THE SACRED DUGONG

We are swimming with masks, wetsuits, and cameras just off the black-sand beach of Ambrym when a light-colored object appears in the very clear water and descends from the surface and begins to slowly probe the seabed with the end of its nose. It is a dugong or sea cow, the first that we have ever had the opportunity to observe! We knew that there were dugong in the Vanuatu islands, but we did not dare hope to see one so unexpectedly and so near us, within just a few yards. We slowly swim in its direction until we are right over it. It has a sort of trunk with which it seems to sniff the seabed and nibble on seaweed, alternating with black pebbles. Its enormous body is more than 9 ft (2.5 m) long and the movement of the water reveals its rings of fat. Two pilot fish are its constant companions. The dugong inches slowly over the black volcanic sea bottom, raising small clouds of sand on either side of its "trunk." It then pushes off and rises upward towards us until it reaches the water's surface to breathe, taking in a couple of mouthfuls of air and splashing playfully like a dolphin. We remain still and indecisive, not daring even to snap a picture for fear that the click will reveal our presence and frighten it away. Its fatty "spare tires" shake as it breathes deeply, getting enough air into its lungs to dive back down to the seabed. It seems to be unaware of our presence, perhaps because we are backlit, perhaps due to blindness, or maybe it does not care.

We dive back down to find it still there, nibbling, quite oblivious to everything else. Evidently, this is mealtime and nothing and no one could spoil that for the sea cow. Every once in a while it rises to breathe then descends again, moving away from its previous spot by just a few yards each time. When we find it again the second time, we decide that it is time to become better friends and swim down very slowly until we are right next to it, stretching out a hand in an attempt to touch this beautiful creature. The sea cow swerves slightly, looks at us, and moves away with determination, swimming along the seabed with surprising speed that is unexpected for its size. We try to follow but its majestic white silhouette disappears and the sea floor beneath us turns into an unchanging stretch of black.

PACIFIC OCEAN

131

132-133 The Rom dance is practiced by the men in the mountain villages who make their straw clothing and colored wooden masks especially for this occasion.

133 top The central core of Vanuatu community life is the nakamal, which is a clearing just outside the village with a gigantic banana tree in the middle.

133 center The ating ating are tomtoms in the form of totem poles that can be up to 20 ft (6 m) in height with carved human-like heads that recall ancestors.

133 bottom A rudimentary concrete oven fueled by wood takes its place alongside the traditional techniques of cooking over a fire or in an underground pit.

Ambrym

134 bottom right Anuta was renamed Cherry Island by the English because of its round shape that makes it look like a cherry and its long isthmus as the stem.

135 bottom The whole island is surrounded by a coral barrier, where powerful oceanic waves break, protecting its shores from the effects of the sea.

134-135 Like the ancient Polynesians, the natives of Anuta know how to push their canoes past the coral reef breakers in order to fish.

134 bottom left It is with these simple dark stones driven into the white sand that the inhabitants of Anuta remember their dead.

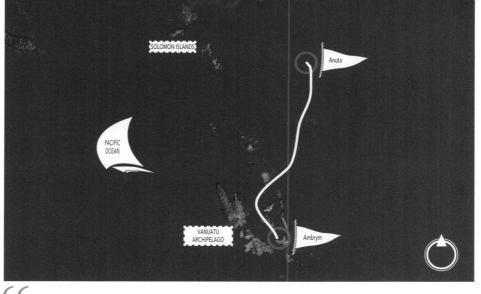

> *280 Miles. Five days of journeying through some headwinds to reach a very small island, far away from any other land. Anchoring is difficult, disembarking dangerous, but we are welcomed on land with traditional Polynesian hospitality.*

Anuta

THE LAST POLYNESIAN ENCLAVE

At the end of the white line on the horizon we catch sight of a number of short vertical lines. They are, in fact, the natives of Anuta who have been crowding onto the beach, waiting for us to arrive. Three canoes launch into the sea, crossing the breakers and moving nearer us. They shout out something, move toward the prow of our boat, and guide us along the leeward side towards a relatively calm area, to the junction between waves coming from the north and south. They lead us to a sandy area and we drop anchor, even though the seabed is too high for a secure anchorage and all around us there are coral crags and boulders, and even though the boat is rolling miserably. A canoe flanks us, a man jumps aboard, and hands us a damp piece of paper signed by the island's elders. It says that we are welcome here, that we may stay as long as we like, and that their people would like us to disembark on their land. Attempting to disembark via our dinghy would be crazy, so the man invites us to take a seat in the canoe. The island's perimeter is battered by waves that are several yards high. When we reach the last of the breakers, the rowers slow down and wait, looking over their shoulders. They count the waves … and then the rower at the stern gives the signal and everyone begins to paddle quickly and powerfully. The canoe darts forward and flies over the water as an enormous breaker forms in front of the prow. We move at the same speed as we soar into the hollow taking shape just after the crest of the wave and while the next one is forming aft. When it arrives and raises us, it is strong enough to throw us into the air, as we again take flight suspended on the crest, though not strong enough to capsize us. We fly along on the spray and foam for a few yards more, pushed along by the wave and oars, we enter into the wave's hollow, and land roughly on the coral flat. When we jump onto land, another wave washes over us from head to foot.

Anuta is an unpolluted gem, protected by the enormous expanse of choppy sea that makes getting here difficult and leaving just as harrowing an experience. Everything on the island is natural and unspoilt. Nothing is imported from outside the island. There are no plastic containers, no electricity, no radio or television, not even nets for fishing or pots for cooking. More people await our arrival on the beach. We have to shake everyone's hand and there are more than 100 people here! All except for the chief, as he remains behind to wait for us, sitting upright on a mat at the extreme end of the village. To greet him, we must approach on our knees so that we will be at his height and hold out our hands, moving our noses near his, following the ancient Polynesian custom. We offer him our gifts of an aluminum soup tureen with onions, garlic, a kilo (about 2.2 lb) of sugar, a packet of matches, some fishhooks, an old pipe, and Fijian tobacco. He is satisfied with them and in exchange offers us a mat and dismisses us. We are now free to explore the village, free to film and photograph a way of life that seems to be from the time of Captain Cook. We are allowed to scale the only 214-ft (65-m) high hill and to view from above the island's entirety, this little plot of land in the midst of an ocean that has for 20 generations been home to a small handful of Polynesians so far removed from the outside world.

136 top left The mail boat arrives only once per year, compelling inhabitants to learn how to live using exclusively what the island produces.

136 top right The bright orange achieved with the curcuma (turmeric) powder dissolved in coconut oil is the paint with which they adorn themselves on festival days.

136 bottom Huts on Anuta are so low that you cannot stand up inside, however, because of their height they are quite resistant to damage from cyclones.

Anuta

136-137 On Anuta, there are no metal pots, just traditional wooden containers and food is cooked by being arranged among very hot stones.

137 bottom Although the island is politically a part of the Melanesian Solomon Islands, its inhabitants are Polynesians who came here 15 generations ago following a long migration by canoe.

138-139 It was perhaps on this remote island that, following the shipwreck of the Astrolabe, the enlightened aspirations and dreams of La Pérouse and his expedition ended.

138 bottom The water inside this bay is calm and greenish in color due to the dark green reflections of the shores covered in a dense layer of forest and mangroves.

139 bottom The Solomon Islands were a British protectorate until 1978 when they became an independent country with Honiara as their capital.

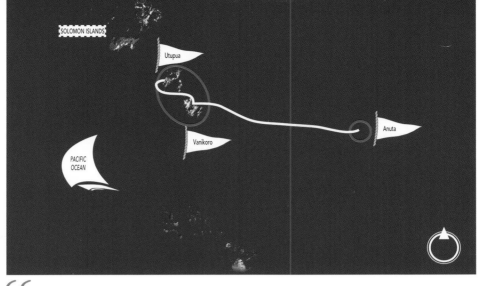

" *250 Miles. Three days pass and we enter the shelter of a lagoon at an island that looks uninhabited.* "

Vanikoro and Utupua Islands
MEN WITH RED TEETH

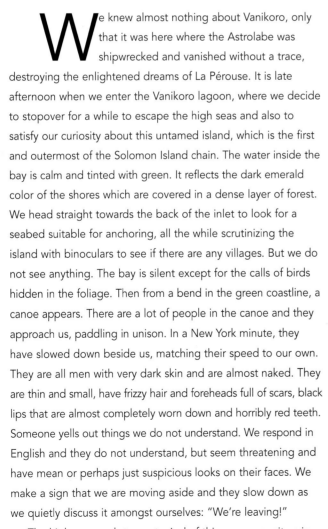

We knew almost nothing about Vanikoro, only that it was here where the Astrolabe was shipwrecked and vanished without a trace, destroying the enlightened dreams of La Pérouse. It is late afternoon when we enter the Vanikoro lagoon, where we decide to stopover for a while to escape the high seas and also to satisfy our curiosity about this untamed island, which is the first and outermost of the Solomon Island chain. The water inside the bay is calm and tinted with green. It reflects the dark emerald color of the shores which are covered in a dense layer of forest. We head straight towards the back of the inlet to look for a seabed suitable for anchoring, all the while scrutinizing the island with binoculars to see if there are any villages. But we do not see anything. The bay is silent except for the calls of birds hidden in the foliage. Then from a bend in the green coastline, a canoe appears. There are a lot of people in the canoe and they approach us, paddling in unison. In a New York minute, they have slowed down beside us, matching their speed to our own. They are all men with very dark skin and are almost naked. They are thin and small, have frizzy hair and foreheads full of scars, black lips that are almost completely worn down and horribly red teeth. Someone yells out things we do not understand. We respond in English and they do not understand, but seem threatening and have mean or perhaps just suspicious looks on their faces. We make a sign that we are moving aside and they slow down as we quietly discuss it amongst ourselves: "We're leaving!"

The high seas and storms typical of this season await us in the open sea, but waves seem to be the least of our worries at the moment. Thus without attempting any further dialogue, we alter our course by 180° and head for the inlet entrance through which we have just come. The canoe stops as their eyes silently follow as we move out of the inlet. We come out of the inlet at dusk and for the whole night we must constantly change sail and alter our route in order to avoid more serious problems. At dawn and 60 miles (100 km) further away, another island appears, Utupua. It also has a large bay with dark waters and shores covered in greenery. People also travel out to meet us upon our arrival, not one but two canoes full of small men, also with red teeth. But because it is morning and because we could not possibly sail any further, they look less menacing to us so we drop anchor. It is our first encounter with the Melanesian people of the Solomon Islands, men with savage-looking faces but with gentle souls. They are a timid people who always introduce themselves with their heads lowered and reserved looks, people that we mistook for having a cruel air about them.

140-141 Lateral planking doesn't just serve as a place to print the name of the boat but also as protection for the cockpit against unexpected splashing water.

140 bottom Just after dropping anchor in the bay, a procession of canoes arrives alongside our boat to greet us, chat, and offer us the best that the lagoon produces.

141 bottom We offer towels, old sheets, and T-shirts in order to satisfy the inhabitants' desire for lengths of fabric to be used as sarongs.

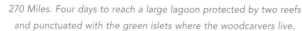

" *270 Miles. Four days to reach a large lagoon protected by two reefs and punctuated with the green islets where the woodcarvers live.* "

The Marovo Lagoon
THE CARVERS OF NGUZUNGUZU

Money is useless in the lagoon at Marovo. The capital of Honiara is only about 100 miles (160 km) away, but far enough away for no kind of money exchange to exist. One hundred miles to go and sell products, and just as many to return with purchases are too many to travel by canoe, so the inhabitants of this lagoon prefer to wait until someone comes to them and then to barter their products for whatever they need in return. We were informed of this practice and also knew that in Marovo's lagoon there are ebony woodcarvers. They sculpt the wood that grows in the hills of Vangunu Island in the middle of the lagoon. It is a dark ebony wood with lighter grains that give finished pieces a luminous marbleized effect. The lagoon's artisans have been carving ebony for centuries and are famous for their masterly reproductions of the most important figures in their local tradition, the *nguzunguzu*. They are anthropomorphic figures that are installed at the prow of boats and whose presence recalls the nature of their expeditions. If the human effigy holds a fish or another animal in its hand, it means that the people on board the canoe, at times dozens, are going out to fish or hunt. If the *nguzunguzu* holds a human head then it means that the expedition is going out to hunt human beings and you need to hide or get ready for a fight. This documented and brutal custom actually endured until the first decades of the 19th century.

Just after we drop anchor in the bay, a procession of canoes arrives alongside our boat to greet us, chat, and offer us the best that the lagoon produces: pineapples, bananas, bunches of coconuts, pumpkins, and also fish, crabs, even a very beautiful electric blue butterfly, and naturally the *nguzunguzu* and other ebony objects. We barter with what we have on board: fishhooks, flour, cookies, rice, tea, and sugar. After several days, we are able get the natives to understand that we do not have

a refrigerator for all of the fish they want to offer us, while they have an intense desire for sarongs or just lengths of fabric. We remedy the situation by offering some towels, old sheets, and T-shirts, and the exchanges continue.

One morning, a canoe arrives carrying a little old man with a stack of ebony logs. The man makes us understand that he wants to give us one of the logs in exchange for our little speedboat. However, this is not an exchange we can make! Although our little speedboat is old and beat up, it is indispensable to us. Without it, we could not move around in the lagoon or even reach land anywhere on our travels. The old man does not give in and offers us a second log then a third. Given the value of that ebony in Italy, we could buy three new little speedboats, but that battered craft is more useful and valuable to us right now. The little old man loses his bearings. He offers us more wood, making us understand that he can give us as much as we would like! We give him gifts of a T-shirt and a sack of sugar. We watch him move away, resigned, paddling slowly in his canoe loaded with valuable ebony wood logs.

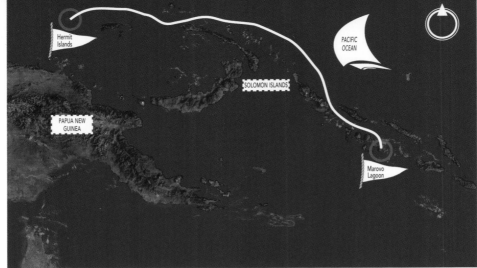

"
900 Miles. Ten days of anxiety-ridden sailing along the difficult coast of Papua New Guinea to reach a place inhabited by 100 people that live in an idyllic world.
"

The Hermit Islands

A PARADISE IN THE MIDDLE OF THE SEA

Perhaps the Garden of Eden was only a little better than what we see in front of us, where the only village on the Hermit atoll is scattered across two green hills joined by a stretch of grassy plain, with the waters lapping at its shores. Huts stand peacefully along the grassy stretch, built with sago palm fronds, raised up off of the ground and surrounded by coconut palms, papaya and mango trees, and flowering bushes. The Polynesian good nature of the inhabitants is also in perfect harmony with the landscape as the people are smiling, welcoming, and generous. On the ground, several women are intent upon cooking and when the meal is ready, there is food for everyone, including any passersby. The men cultivate farms on the hills and return with truckloads of pineapples, pumpkins, sweet potatoes, and sugar cane. On moonless nights, men and women go fishing, guiding their canoes through the tranquil waters of the atoll. In the dark, you can hear their songs and calls, as well as the fish jumping, attracted by the diffuse light of their lanterns. In the sea as on the land, there are abundant food sources here. There is enough for

everyone, even for us, and until just a few days ago we did not even know that this remote atoll existed, just 100 miles (160 km) north of Papua New Guinea. Every time that we return to the dinghy, we find some produce, a smoked fish filet, or some tubers, and we do not even know how to thank them. "Someone put it there. It's a tenth of the harvest that is served to the needy or to guests," they say. Children play in the water and play tag on the grass, climb the palm trees, and paddle canoes. You can hear singing everywhere. Maybe this minuscule yet marvelous spot, inhabited by just 140 souls, is truly heaven on earth. However, it was not always that way. We learn about it when Joseph, the head of the community, insists on telling us the history of the atoll. "Many people once lived here, all of the islands in the atoll were inhabited, and one village would often war with another. At times, captured enemies were eaten. Then one day, the first ship full of white people arrived. All of the inhabitants of the atoll came to an agreement and ended up welcoming the new arrivals in friendship, but once night fell, they swam out to the ship, went on board, killed everyone, and set everything on fire, stealing only one copper pot from the ship." As confirmation that all of this is true, Joseph shows us an oxidized pot with holes in it that the island chiefs have handed down from father to son so that all would remember the history he is now recounting to us. After the first ship, others arrived and all came to the same end until one survivor successfully reached the coast of New Guinea in a canoe and organized an expedition of retaliation. "In the end, a ship of armed men came here. Many of us died, those that survived made peace with the white men and all of the inhabitants here united in one sole village. From that time forward, peace has reigned here and when one of us goes to New Guinea, he or she is welcomed in friendship while the same happens when someone comes here from another place."

142 bottom A punctured and oxidized pot that the chiefs on the island handed down from father to son is all that remains of the first ship of white people who disembarked here.

143 Two green hills united by a grassy plain with calm water lapping at both sides of the atoll. Perhaps the Garden of Eden was not so different to this place.

144-145 A treacherous watery maze more than 1,000 miles (1,600 km) long, but nevertheless still splendid with the most intense turquoise and sky blue colors that you could ever imagine.

144 bottom Attracted by the current that runs east or west according to the time of day, dolphins arrive by the thousands to escort us along our passage among the coral.

145 bottom In the transparent water beneath the keel, there is an incredible universe of colorful fish and coral – the largest natural aquarium on the planet.

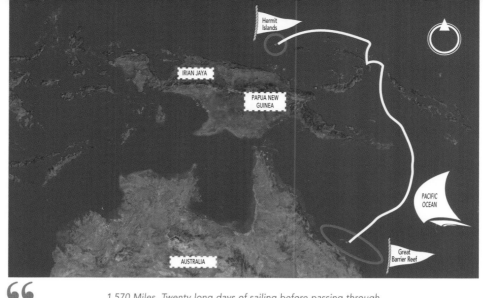

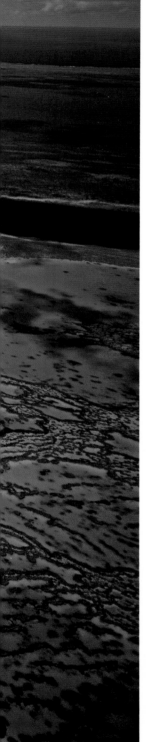

> 1,570 Miles. Twenty long days of sailing before passing through the labyrinth of the Solomon Islands then on across the ocean with a headwind to arrive at a wall of coral the length of a continent.

The Great Barrier Reef

CORAL IN THE MIDDLE OF THE SEA

It was 11 p.m. on 11 June, 1770 when the *Endeavour*, commanded by Captain Cook coming from Botany Bay en route north, ground to a halt against a sudden obstacle. The ship started taking on water and 24 hours passed before the legendary skill of its commander, aided by a fortunate combination of wind and tide, successfully freed it. It took five days to reach the Australian coast just a few dozen leagues away and once there the Englishmen noticed that a large coral mass had remained stuck in the ship's planking, thereby preventing them from sinking to the sea floor. This was the first close encounter that a European ship had ever had with the Australian Great Barrier Reef. More than 3,000 coral formations and not less than 1,000 islands stretching for almost 1,616 miles (2,600 km) off the coast of Queensland. This is an immense structure, the largest in the world built by living organisms, and is visible to the naked eye from outer space.

Our first encounter with the Great Barrier Reef was from a plane. Just after leaving the Australian coast, light-colored areas appeared in the dark blue sea, like a rash in the ocean, a mountain chain that had collapsed millennia ago, still trying desperately to maintain its existence above the waves. A hazardous maze for those who sail through it without knowing it well. An unforgiving place, yes, but also a magnificent natural phenomenon with the most intense turquoise and sky blues that you could ever imagine. When we reach the reef in our boat, more than two centuries had already passed since Cook's first passage through here, centuries during which this vast living landscape has been thoroughly mapped, surveyed, and photographed, with every detail noted and secret recess probed. With all of this information available, sailing near the Great Barrier Reef today should be easier. However, though the GPS clearly indicates the narrows and though the most minute

detailed coral formations are marked on the map, there are still 200 years' of known and unknown shipwrecks to contend with, reason enough for us to sail with all senses on alert.

When coming in from the ocean, there are neither any markers nor points of reference. At one spot, a barrier appears on the horizon, where the waves that have been driven by the trade winds unobstructed for thousands of miles crash against the reef. It is an impressive spectacle that is always an alarming prospect because waves, winds, and currents all collectively flow in the direction of the reefs. Only when we are very near them, are we able to distinguish a route that will allow us to successfully pass through. Beyond this passage, the sea suddenly calms and we can stop, anchoring in the sandy seabeds on the leeward side of this massive wall of coral. The barrier reef rises up at quite a distance from the coast along the whole length of the horizon around us, and we do not see the mast of another boat or any land, but beneath the keel there is an incredible universe of color, fish, and coral in the transparent water, the largest natural aquarium on the planet.

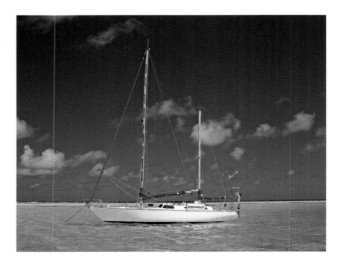

The Great Barrier Reef

146 top left and bottom
The contribution of fresh clean water coming from the ocean guarantees coral colonies the optimal conditions for thriving.

146 top right
The Ginglymostoma cirratum, or nurse shark, is a harmless animal that feeds on the calamari, octopi, and small fish commonly found around coral reefs.

146-147 and 147 bottom right
Entering by way of one of the channels, the sea suddenly calms and we can stopover wherever we like, anchoring on the sandy seabeds leeward of the coral bank.

147 bottom left In the lives of young sea turtles, the most dangerous moment occurs once they have come out of their shells and have to journey over the strip of beach that separates them from the sea.

146

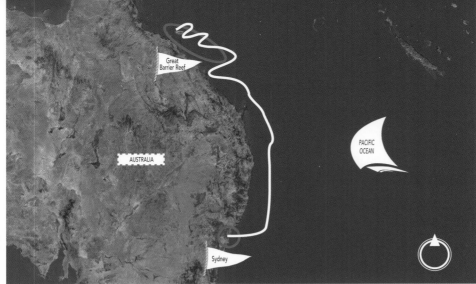

Great
Barrier Reef

AUSTRALIA

PACIFIC
OCEAN

Sydney

" *1,140 Miles. Eleven days without stopping along a route that, with the increasing latitudes, offers colder and stronger winds with progressively more difficult seas to conquer.* "

Sydney

SAILING INTO THE FUTURE

The Sydney Opera House is one of the great architectural icons of our time. Its conch-shaped roofs, similar to the sections of nautilus shell, vary in form and appearance as we gradually approach in the boat. Their color changes from white to pink, to grey and yellow according to the position of the sun. A jewel shaped by humans looking out over a jewel of land and water cut by nature.

When in 1788 the English, in search of a safe place to found a colony, entered this natural port on the east coast of Australia, they had no doubts about what they had found. A bay opened up in front of them with so many miles of coastline slotted with numerous inlets where ships could find refuge from any sort of wind or sea. There was abundant fresh water, fertile land, and green hills as far

as the eye could see. They christened the area Port Jackson and founded Sydney, the oldest Australian city. It is the oldest but now also the most populous and modern with a great deal of exciting architecture as well as the Opera House, such as the futuristic skyscrapers of downtown, the ANP Tower, the tallest building in the southern hemisphere, and, not forgetting, the equally iconic Harbour Bridge joining the south and north sides of the bay.

Sydney is perhaps not exactly the typical destination for sea vagabonds. Searching for the most distant, least well-known, and least visited places is really our aim, but just after rounding the low promontory of South Bay and entering Port Jackson, we feel complete awe. Arriving by sea is by far the best way to appreciate the beauty of the natural features and the stunning modernity of the city. At the same time you feel partly in the past, seeing the natural wonder that the first Europeans saw, and right in the heart of the 21st century. The bay opening up around us is what hundreds of thousands of deported people, sailors, and immigrants have seen over the centuries – beauty, a safe harbor, and hope for the future.

However, the rivers that had originally attracted the English colonists almost completely ran dry, the pink eucalyptus trees no longer adorned the banks, the Aboriginal villages disappeared, and the ecology of the bay was modified, more or less progressively over time, by human intervention. Motorboats, ships, ferries full of tourists, tugboats, sailboats, small ferry boats, an overwhelming amount of water traffic, and, despite being on a very sheltered bay, treacherous and troublesome waves and crosscurrents are the result for us today. Nevertheless, once anchored safe and sound along with other boats in Port Sydney Marina, we find ourselves enveloped by the peace and calm of this modern yet friendly city, where on land you can move around on foot or by train, and in summer at five p.m. many escape from behind their computers and jump onto their surfboards. You can walk just a few hundred yards and hear ten different languages spoken and enjoy the cuisine of just as many countries. In Sydney, you have the impression of a place that bridges the past and the future, between old Europe and the multiethnic society of centuries to come.

148 bottom Even for those who sail out in search of yet unknown cultures and unspoilt nature, a fully equipped shipyard is a luxury not to be shunned.

148-149 A jewel built by humans lies over a jewel of a bay formed by nature. The Sydney Opera House is one of the architectural icons of our time.

149 bottom It is a great feeling to arrive through the same port of entry that for 250 years served thousands of people all in search of new lives and better futures.

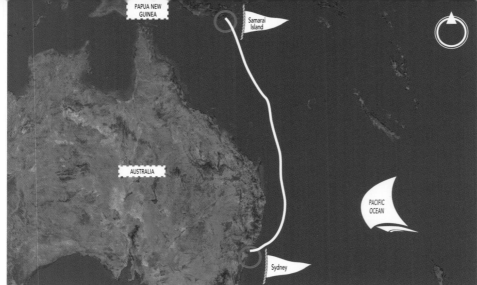

PAPUA NEW GUINEA

Samarai Island

AUSTRALIA

PACIFIC OCEAN

Sydney

" *1,550 Miles. Two weeks to return to the shelter of the equator on an island where both ancient and modern lifestyles coexist in a manner that at times is bizarre.* "

Samarai Island

A LITTLE THEATER ON THE PIER

Samarai Island is the administrative capital of the eastern district of Papua New Guinea. Given its importance, we were expecting a crowded city with a lot of movement and packed markets. But it isn't at all like that. It is a small and sleepy town with just three streets, a few dozen houses, an old colonial period hotel, and a dilapidated theater. Upon our arrival, a customs officer and policeman were fishing from the pier and after stamping our passports they go back to their fishing as if it were their job. The town seems to live in slow motion with the little activity centered around a general store that is the only one in the town, on the island, and maybe in the district. However, something happens on our fourth day here. We already perceive that something new is stirring in the morning as a general reawakening occurs. People are on the streets, there are new faces, and there is movement and expectation. On the pier, unusually dressed up

women begin to gather, wearing traditional straw skirts. Then the reason for all the bustle appears, a passenger ship arrives to discharge a horde of Australian tourists onto the pier. When the first tourist sets foot on the pier, T-shirts and flip-flops disappear, revealing bared breasts and straw skirts, then the women begin to dance and sing following the music of two drummers, also appearing out of the blue. The scene is impressive with throaty voices, thunderous drums, and dark-skinned, shiny bodies smeared with coconut oil. The very white tourists, all wearing sunglasses and straw hats, find it hard to believe their eyes and collect their memories with humming video cameras and a series of camera flashes. Further along, a group of men and women also outfitted in traditional dress, grate the trunk of a sago palm tree. The sawdust pours into a wooden container of running water then passes through a filter of coconut fiber. Everyone works in unison, singing a monotonous tune that keeps rhythm with the event, but once the last tourist turns the corner they stop and stretch out in the shade to smoke. Not far away, a family grates cassava and coconut, wrapping the paste up in banana leaves, while stones are gathered for the pit barbecue. On another corner, two women wash their newborn babies, ladling water from a wooden container with coconut halves. Once immortalized on film, all of these people ask for a tip that is never denied as it is a small price for these incredulous tourists who are able to capture such intense, natural, and authentic images! The show is interrupted at noon when the Australians disappear into the hotel, but starts up again in the afternoon and continues until the last tourist returns to the ship. Then everyone changes back to everyday clothes and life on Samarai continues as always. We all feel very disappointed, because this is not what we were hoping to find in Papua! Months later, we would discover that sago eaters still exist and that traditional ceremonies have not completely vanished. However to find them, you must travel a great distance upriver or to the most outlying islands, certainly not encounter them in the capital cities.

150 bottom On a sailboat there are several dozen lines, all with a different function and name of its own. This one is the jib sheet.

150-151 Canoes carved from tree trunks are still today the most widespread means of transport for longer voyages along the island's perimeter and the coastline.

151 bottom In 1975, Papua New Guinea, a union between the British New Guinea colony and German Papua, became an independent country with its capital at Port Moresby.

152-153 The Torres Strait is a natural channel dotted with thousands of low-lying islets and an incalculable number of coral reefs connecting the Pacific to the Indian Ocean.

152 bottom The waters in the strait are international, you may anchor wherever you like but you may not get out on dry land before going through customs in Australia.

153 bottom Beacons and other signaling devices indicate the route to take, but keeping an eye out from above never hurts. The labyrinth of islands here and rocks require careful attention.

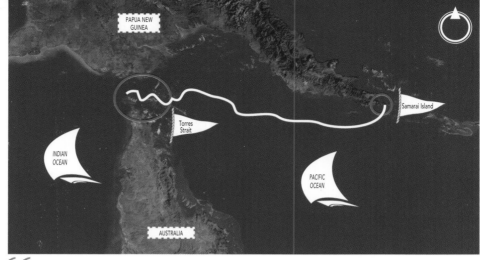

"500 Miles. Five days and then we enter a complicated and contorted natural channel, a place of contrasts between uncontaminated islands, heavy water traffic, dangerous shallows, and schools of sea turtles."

The Torres Strait

BOUNDARY BETWEEN TWO WORLDS

The beam of the Bramble Cay lighthouse clearly signals our entry into the Torres Strait, a natural channel full of thousands of low islets and an incalculable number of coral reefs, which constitutes the route between the northernmost point of Australia and southernmost point of Papua New Guinea. We are now traveling from the Pacific Ocean to the Indian Ocean. The Torres Strait is a strange place, a 150-mile (240-km) maze that both unites and divides distant and diverse worlds. To the north, Papua lives in the past with straw-hut villages and recent memories of the last headhunters. The ordered and rich cities of Australia to the south live in the future. The immense open spaces of the Pacific lie in the east and the very densely populated coasts of the Indian Ocean to the west.

A coast guard plane appears, heading straight for us. The pilot rocks the wings of the plane, indicating that we must turn on our VHF radio and respond to a series of questions, which include who we are, where we are coming from, where we are heading, do we intend to stopover in Australia and if so, where and why. They thank us in the end but we still feel like they have been spying on us. There is no wind and we proceed with our motor on throughout the night, having faith in the coastal signal lights, which unlike those on the islands in the Pacific are accurate and efficient. There are other ships traveling through the strait and we see examples of all sorts of light sources as reported in the manuals: area beacons, tugboat lights, pilot lights, lights from anchored ships, lights from ships moving slowly, and lights from ships towing other ships. Around us, we constantly hear calls from the coast guard on the VHF, asking for information and explanations. We miss the silence and solitude of the Pacific where we never had to think about nighttime sailing through coral reefs and islets. The sun rises, it quickly gets hot, and winds are nonexistent. Low seabeds and many islets invite us to drop anchor and rest for a while. But, what is there to do here? We boldly call the coast guard and ask permission. Permission granted, we can drop anchor, but we cannot disembark on land for any reason or even enter the water. We first must reach Darwin and go

through customs, immigration, and quarantine! To think, in Polynesia we sometimes had to chase down the customs officer to get him to stamp our passports while he was working on the plantation or roasting a small pig! We abandon the main route, enter a secondary channel, and drop anchor just off of a barren island with mucky water that we imagine is infested with crocodiles, stinging jellyfish, and poisonous polyps as described in the guidebooks. But at first glance, we have to change our minds. Amazingly, we are soon surrounded by dozens of sea turtles, besieging the boat, snorting, and craning their necks to see what we are doing. They watch us for a while then submerge slowly to reemerge 40 feet (12 m) further away. This happens throughout the day and for part of the night while we stopover waiting for some wind. It is almost as if they know that we are prohibited from entering the water to join them.

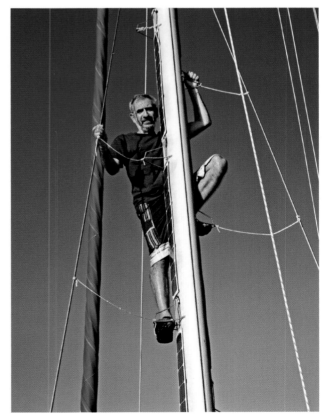

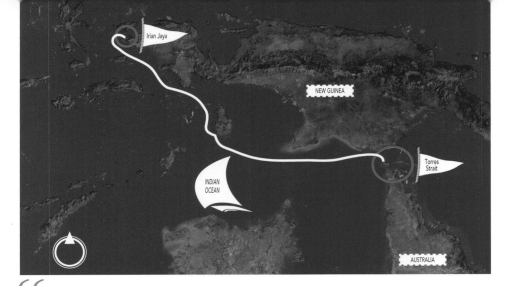

" *970 Miles. Ten days and a dive into the past among deep bays where inhabitants of hidden villages still fish using ancient techniques.* "

Irian Jaya

FISHING WITH POISON

The colors are intense, the mountains inaccessible, and the forest primeval. Even the sea is strange. There is not a wave to be seen and the water's glassy surface reflects mountains and motionless clouds. We seem to be living inside a Japanese watercolor, but we are not in Japan, we are in Irian Jaya on one of the biggest, deepest, and most distant of bays. It is an incredibly different world, as far away from our own as is the earth from the moon. It is an enormous area with high mountains and deep valleys dense with unspoilt forests, with no roads or vehicles, nothing that reminds us we are living in the 21st century.

The small town facing our anchorage spot is called Kaprus, which consists of about 20 pile-dwellings reflected on the still waters of the immense bay. About a dozen canoes have come out to us and hang around the hull of our boat as we anchor. There are many people in them and communication is quite difficult. Even though we are officially in Indonesia, no one here understands our few words of Indonesian. Our hosts are very shy, stop about a dozen yards away and remain there for hours, immobile, watching us. However, as time passes, they start to understand us and within just a few days we are at a home in the village. We film the fishermen that hunt sea turtles with bows and arrows and hunters returning with small marsupials captured around the village.

As we fished with them we observed an ancient technique that we have never witnessed before. The men plunge into the water to explore the clefts and caves among the rocks. In order to scan the seabeds, they use only a pair of small wooden goggles, staying underwater for a very long time, searching, watching, and patrolling. When one of them locates a fish in its hiding place, he returns to the canoe, tears off a root, "tenderizes" it with a hammer, dives back in, then when he reaches the fish he stretches into where it is hiding, opens his hand and frees the juice from the root, which tints the water with its cloudy and milky consistency. After just a few seconds, the fish emerges from its lair dazed, disoriented, and unable to swim and the fisherman easily grabs it and brings it to the surface. The substance responsible for this is rotenone, a poison naturally present in the roots of the Derris *elliptica* plant. This toxin is innocuous to warm-blooded animals so is not harmful to adults and children, but it is deadly to cold-blooded animals, requiring only a few drops to paralyze the respiratory system of fish.

In the western world, this kind of fishing is prohibited because this poison is also toxic to millions of microorganisms that live in coral reefs. Yet here, it is used moderately and only for providing food. A balance between the sizable lagoons and the large numbers of inhabitants feeding on their fish has evidently been achieved in a time-tested equilibrium that is still sustainable today.

154 bottom Their lives depend
on the sea and these people live
the major part of their lives on it,
indifferent to the impassable
mountains that rise up behind
their village. Kaprus is a village
of about 20 pile dwellings at the
back of the largest bay on the
northern coast of Irian Jaya.

154-155 On the large jagged
gulfs that notch the Irian Jaya
coastline, the sea is strangely
calm with no hint of waves,
almost as if it were a lake.

155 bottom Fishermen at Kaprus
are capable of diving and
remaining in the water for long
periods of time. Equipped only
with small wooden goggles, they
capture their prey by stunning
them with a natural poison.

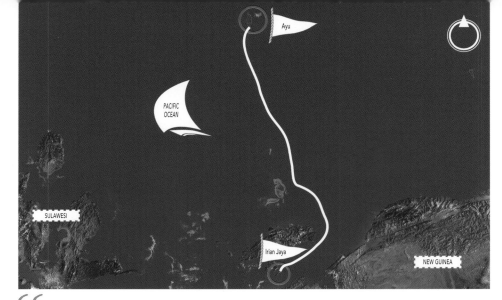

> 330 Miles. Three days to arrive at a self-sufficient microcosm with a population that has adapted perfectly to life in the midst of the ocean.

Ayu

BETWEEN INDONESIA AND THE PHILIPPINES

The little girl sees something in the sand, slides the small stick to a depth of about five inches then starts to dig around the area, sinking her arm to the elbow she begins to pull slowly without ever giving up. Her hand reemerges with fingers clenching a kind of whitish earthworm, about one foot long and as thick as her thumb. We are on an enormous sandbank, exposed by low tide, with a surface corrugated by parallel wrinkles among which puddles of seawater form, inhabited by a great number of creatures, such as light-colored starfish, perfectly mimicking

the white sand's surface, mollusks moving just beneath the surface and leaving a telltale straight path, and strange tubular organisms that drill through the sand creating small spiral tunnels. For us, this sandbank is a mine full of spectacular images, but for the inhabitants of the atoll it is just a place where they go to hunt for food, where women and children come, all searching for the white worms.

Worm-hunting continues until the tide is too low, the water completely retreats, and the strange annelids take refuge deep below, so deep that their siphons are no longer visible on the surface. The women then get back into their canoes, hoist sails, and head towards the circle of palm trees on a distant island. We follow them and disembark at one of the four villages on the atoll. Around each dwelling is everything that the family possesses, pandanus mats, pots, a small fire pit, fishing equipment, and a few hens. We discover that the atoll does not have contact with the outside world, except for a few Philippine fishing boats and one other boat that comes from Irian Jaya once a month if the sea is calm. Thus, our appearance is an event that arouses great curiosity from what we can see.

Clusters of worms, meanwhile, end up on a grill along with others that are already cooked, looking like golden tree branches. They offer us some and we have to taste them, they are tough and we have to bite down on them and pull hard to get them into chewable pieces, but the flavor is pleasant, tasting much like squid. White worms are a special dish for holidays. The people collect them on Friday and Saturday so that they will have plenty for Sunday dinner. The thickest worms are smoked and set aside, to be used as currency when the ship comes from the coast because in Irian Jaya they are also considered a delicacy.

156 bottom To preserve the octopi, they are left to dry under the sun.

156-157 The atoll of Ayu has no contact with the rest of the world except for one boat that comes from Irian Jaya once a month.

157 bottom left Smoked Sipunculids (peanut worms) constitute a dish for very special days.

157 bottom right On Ayu two blacksmiths are forging machetes.

158-159 Reefing to reduce the surface of the mainsail when wind increases only looks like a complicated maneuver.

160 bottom right Before arriving in Indonesia, you must obtain a navigation permit valid for three months, a regulatory remnant left behind by the old colonial regime.

161 bottom Once known as the Spice Islands, and the cause of many battles and wars for their control, the Moluccas are now part of Indonesia.

160-161 Whether from a natural viewpoint or an ethnic one, the Moluccas may be considered a zone of transition between Asia and Melanesia.

160 bottom left Three small fishing boats used for shark hunting are docked in the port of Ambon, which is the administrative seat of the district.

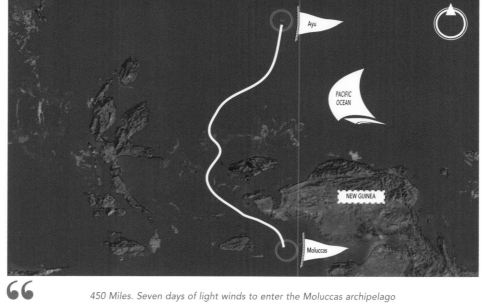

" *450 Miles. Seven days of light winds to enter the Moluccas archipelago composed of hundreds of islands where many villages survive thanks to the sago palm.* "

The Moluccas

SAGO EATERS

They do not eat rice in the Moluccas, instead they eat sago extracted from a special palm tree that grows on the marshy seashores. Before our arrival on Roma Island, we did not really understand which part of the palm was edible. Now we know that the *Metroxylon sagu* is the only sago palm whose trunk is edible, and unlike the slender fresh trunk of sugar cane, it is the thick tough trunk of a 50-ft (15-m) tall, mature tree that is used. However, to be able to eat it you must submit it to a long and elaborate process.

The sago palm grows quickly and in ten years is already very tall, beginning to ripen its first, enormous, and only fruit. It is only through growing this fruit that the trunk produces a great quantity of starch. The tree is cut down when the fruit is still germinating and is left on the tree, while the starch is collected from the trunk. There are two women grating pieces of the trunk just a few yards from the shore when we disembark into our dinghy on the bay at Roma Island. For hours they grind the trunk into huge pieces, leaving a pile of damp, whitish sawdust. When they are finished, the women begin to wash the sawdust in a stream of running water. The channeled stream-water system is beautiful and ingenious, with numerous stalks of bamboo held in position by stakes and liana vines. It diverts fresh water to a spot where they can process the starch from the sago palm trunks. The water bath is filtered through a jute sack stretched across an old wooden canoe, then left to settle all night. The next morning, a kind of "vanilla pudding" is left deposited on the bottom of the canoe and the women collect it, scraping the walls of the canoe until the last remnants are harvested.

This "pudding" is sago "flour" that can be cooked immediately when wet or dried in the sun and kept in palm frond containers, where it can be preserved for months.

Naturally, we have to try some! They prepare little pieces of soft flatbread for us, cooked on red-hot griddles, looking very appetizing yet not tasting as good as they look. They are slimy, rubbery, and have no flavor but just a couple of pieces of the flatbread do fill us up anyway. Certainly, rice or wheat-based products taste better to us, but for the inhabitants of these islands where nothing else grows the sago palm is like manna from heaven. One tree will provide enough food to last a family a whole year.

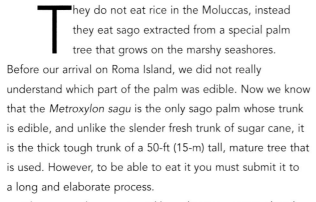

162 top left The whitish mush produced through a long and elaborate process is sago flour and the women scrape the walls of the canoe where it has settled until they get every last bit.

162 top right The water bath is filtered through a jute sack, filling an old wooden canoe, and left to settle over night.

The Moluccas

162 bottom The sago flour may be cooked immediately when wet or left to dry in the sun and preserved for months in containers made from palm fronds.

162-163 After 12 hours they tip the canoe and empty the water until a vanilla pudding-like substance is revealed, deposited in the bottom of the canoe.

163 bottom left To feel full, all you need is a few pieces of soft focaccia flatbread, prepared with sago flour and coconut flakes, and roasted on a red-hot griddle.

163 bottom right Sharing food is the first rule of hospitality throughout the world and the first step towards new friendships. At times, however, it can also be a sacrifice for your hosts.

162

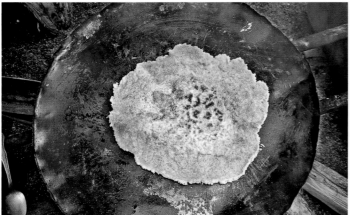

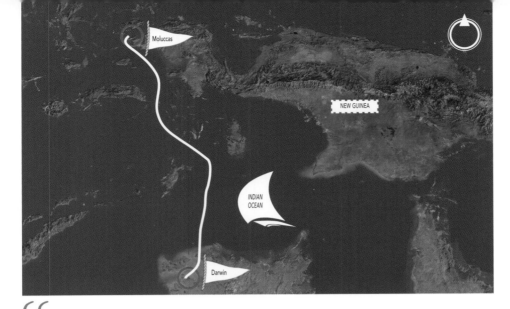

Moluccas

NEW GUINEA

INDIAN OCEAN

Darwin

" *450 Miles. Five days on a sea with impressive tides to arrive at a modern city that has been creatd out of the red Australian desert.* "

Darwin

COEXISTING WITH THE TIDE

e dock at the fishermen's pier, double-knotted to a Vietnamese fishing boat. Thank goodness! Our lines would not have been long enough to dock directly to the jetty. At low tide in Darwin, the water level decreases by 23 ft (7 m), leaving us that far below the pier. Everything at the port is built for this exceptional tidal range. The jetty has stairs that telescope like fire escapes and the pier posts are covered with rubber to avoid wear and tear on lines or damage to the side platings of boats. We disembark at low tide when it becomes an acrobatic maneuver, climbing up on the Vietnamese fishing boat's deckhouse and jumping from there to grab hold of

the last step on the stairway to the pier. Returning to the boat loaded down with full shopping bags is even more difficult, but we learn to choose the right times and adjust all our activities to keep in sync with the tide. Within just a few days, we will use the fishermen's dock, which has to be entered via a lock. However, in order to enter and exit the dock you must first request permission from the lockmaster who is responsible for operating the lock and balancing the water levels.

The ocean waters around Darwin are bizarre. The water is shallow and greenish in color. It is not dirty water, just cloudy due to the effects of the high temperatures that promote the growth of microorganisms. You also have to pay attention because there are potentially deadly crocodiles, sharks, poisonous water snakes, and box jellyfish in these waters. The cloudy water makes it difficult to spot such hazards until the last minute.

We only go back out to sea once to scrub zinc deposits off the keel and other parts of the boat in order to free the screw propeller from a mass of seaweed. We remain out there for as short a time as possible and don't see anything that looks like a shark or a crocodile. Then one day we travel in a local boat up a small river 50 miles (80 km) east of Darwin. We want to see the crocodiles but we never imagined that we would see so many or that they would be so large! They remain still in the muddy water, looking like logs stuck to the riverbed, but when we come within ten feet or so of them they come alive and very quickly dart away. The largest of them can reach about 23 ft (7 m) long and the oldest specimens will even venture into the sea up to several miles away from the coast. Another reason to avoid swimming!

164 bottom Giant termite mounds built with red soil, small hills really, occur frequently along the endless road that connects Darwin to the Australian outback.

164-165 Marshes that form near the mouths of rivers are thriving with aquatic plants and flowers but also contain hiding places for dangerous animals.

165 bottom left For a long time, Darwin was a small outpost of the British Empire, it has grown tremendously now and to tour it you must arrange in advance.

165 bottom right Crocodiles rest immobile like tree trunks in the muddy water, but they come to life and dart away very quickly if you approach them.

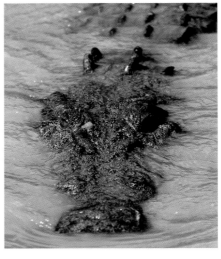

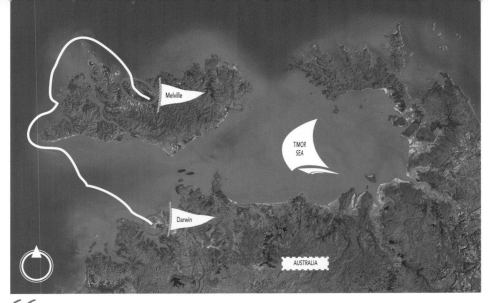

> *170 Miles. Only two days to reach two large islands that, restored to their former owners by the government, are the last refuge for the Tiwi people.*

Bathurst and Melville
ABORIGINAL ISLANDS

The Aborigines gather around the fire, pointing at it and inviting us to sit with them for introductions. "This is Mama Hatty, the most important lady here." The woman wears a threadbare cotton dress and a wool cardigan that is full of holes. She has white hair, yellowed by smoke, skin as black as coal, thin legs, a few missing teeth, and is rolling a cigarette. "She once ate with the Queen Mum," the others exclaim. The group is made up of a dozen people, stretched out or sitting on dirty and singed mattresses. On the fire is an enormous can full of frothy liquid with the head of a sea turtle peeking out of it. Every now and then, someone approaches, tears off a piece of meat and reports that it isn't yet done. The others kill time drinking tea. We sit down with them at 10 a.m. and get back up at sunset. During this whole time, the Aborigines strip meat from the sea turtle's head, stuff themselves with juicy shellfish, drink countless cups of tea with copious amounts of sugar, and smoke any and all tobacco available. Meanwhile, Mama Hatty recounts her story. She is the most important person in this community because she is the first Tiwi, the Aboriginal group that inhabits these islands, to be born from a couple married by priests. "Before, our people didn't know how babies were born.

Every once in a while, women's abdomens swelled and then a baby arrived. Then, we made it so every woman would always have a husband so that the baby would always have a father. A husband was assigned to each baby girl just after her birth and the same was done for each widow the day following the death of her husband. This was our only rule, men and women made love with whomever they desired and, if the woman gave birth to babies, they became the sons and daughters of her existing husband. Then priests came here, said that this was not good and explained what makes up a family, but our people didn't like it. So they promised flour, sugar, and meat to whoever would be married in their church. My father was old, had already outlived two wives, deciding to take advantage of the situation and be married by the priest. I am the first Tiwi child born from this kind of union in marriage."

Contrary to her appearance, Mama Hatty's English is precise and polished. She studied in the white men's schools and for many years was the only schoolteacher on Melville, her island. These circumstances have made her a person of distinction in her community. In the 1960s, she was the companion to the wife of a missionary on the coast. Visiting Australia, the Queen Mother came to find out about this famous and fabled Aboriginal woman, inviting her to lunch. Of course, this increased the aura of legend surrounding the old schoolteacher. Mama Hatty is a woman suspended between two worlds. She proves this again the next day when we run into her near the general store.

"I'm waiting for them to come and pick me up to go to Darwin where there's a meeting of the Aboriginal representatives to the government and I must speak and act on behalf of my community."

"In Darwin, you say? How are you getting there?"

"In an airplane, how else would I get there?"

She travels to Darwin barefoot, wearing her worn dress and holey cardigan, carrying her fabric purse containing shellfish and tobacco, and with a great sense of pride and purpose.

166 bottom The Aborigines weren't aware of how babies were born so they always assigned a husband to every pregnant woman so that a child would always have a father.

166-167 On the shores, you can still see the skeletons of trees and mangroves that toppled during the last tropical storm.

167 bottom left It is estimated that the Aborigines have lived here for more than 30,000 years, but it only took 200 years of European dominion to damage their culture.

167 bottom right Painters in the Tiwi community use colors that recall the landscape where they live, filling their paintings with innumerable small dots to compose images.

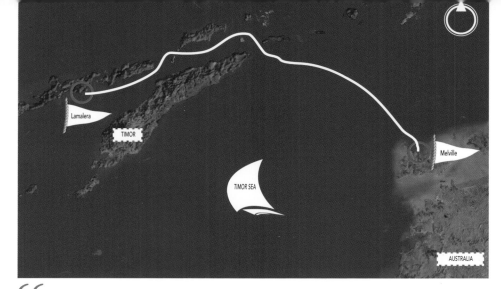

" *550 Miles. Six days, first a small crossing then a delicate navigation through the islands of Nusa Tenggara in order to anchor next to a village that is the only one of its kind in the world.* "

Lamalera

THE LAST WHALE FISHERMEN

At dawn, we are already on the beach with the others pushing the heavy wooden boat into the sea. We jump aboard from the water's edge, as the men grasp the oars and paddle vigorously to cross the breakers. Beyond those breakers, many pairs of strong skilled arms unite in an effort to raise the bamboo mast and hoist the woven screw pine sail that will power the boat for the eight-hour trip. A brief prayer follows the *salamat paghi*, the Indonesian "good day" greeting, and we finally begin the hunt. From May to October this is daily life in Lamalera on the island of Lembata where the last of the whale hunters live.

There are 12 men on board armed with rudimentary harpoons forged in the village from long bamboo poles onto which they attach many spools of threaded rope. Every day for eight hours these men cruise ten miles (16 km) off the coast in hopes of sighting a whale. Other boats from Lamalera are all around us, the *Maria Theresa*, *Saint Theresa*, *Marie of the Sea*, and the *Marisol*, all the same size and made from the same wood as they have

been for the last 1,000 years, with bamboo masts, screw pine woven sails, and large oars used like rudders that two men have to maneuver with all of their strength. We spend hours patrolling the sea with one man stationed at the prow scanning the horizon for a tail, a splash, or simply a sign from one of the other boats. Nothing happens and the sun rises higher and becomes hotter. Someone casts out a fishing line and we catch a sharp-tailed sunfish. They clean it, filet it, and we divide up its very white meat amongst all of us. We eat it just after pulling it in and just as it is, raw, and it feels like gelatin in our mouths, both quenching our thirst and satisfying our hunger. If it weren't for the sharp-tailed sunfish, no one would eat or even drink.

We have been anchored off of Lamalera for one month and every day, except for Sunday, we go out with the hunters, but still there are no traces of any whales. "If we sight a whale," the oldest man, Petrus, tells us, "we pursue it with all of our effort. When we reach it, one man throws his harpoon directly at the whale's back to pierce it effectively. The whale then tries to move to a lower depth, pulling the harpoon and rope with it, sometimes towing the boat for hours, and sometimes even days. When it tires and we can move in closer, men harpoon it then others jump in the water with ropes running everywhere, the whale tosses and turns, blood tints the water, there is a lot of shouting and calling out, and boat prows graze against each other. When the whale stops moving, we tie it to the boat and drag it to the beach. It takes two days to clean and cut it up completely, including the meat, fat, skin, and bones. Then, we divide it up amongst the whole village, using every last drop of oil. Afterward, we have a big celebration."

Over a six-month period and with better weather, they catch only three or four whales. Usually they harpoon whales that are old and sick, so removal of these whales does not endanger the entire species but ensures the survival of the people of Lamalera and upholds their hunting tradition.

168 bottom A man remains stationary at the prow, scanning the horizon to spot a tail, splashing water, or simply a signal from one of the other boats.

169 The boats are all still the same, built just as they were a thousand years ago with a bamboo mast, a sail made from woven pandanus, and a large oar used as a rudder.

Lamalera

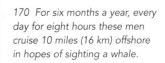

170 For six months a year, every day for eight hours these men cruise 10 miles (16 km) offshore in hopes of sighting a whale.

171 top left At dawn, crews help each other to push their heavy boats from the shore and, once at the water's edge, they all jump on board.

171 center left When the harpooned whale becomes exhausted, the fishermen tie it to the side of their boat, making the concerted and considerable effort to tow it to the beach.

171 bottom left They only harpooned no more than four or five whales a year and the

species is not put at risk while the survival of the people at Lamalera is ensured.

171 right It takes two days to butcher a whale and the meat, fat, skin, bones are divided among the entire village, not wasting even the last drop of oil.

172-173 and 172 bottom The very fragile red coral is eroded and ground up by waves that break at the water's edge, contributing to the formation of the pastel-colored sand on the shore.

173 bottom Crystalline water, colored coral, pink beaches, colonies of bats migrating at sunset, green plains and hills as far as the eye can see, this is the archipelago of Komodo.

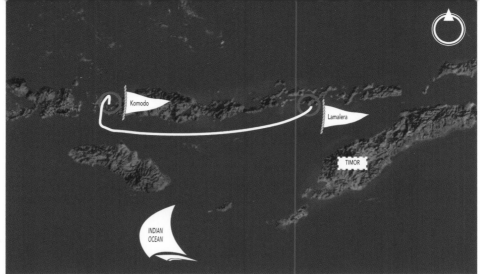

" 240 Miles. Four days following a difficult route
due to violent tidal currents around Komodo. "

Komodo

THE KINGDOM OF THE DRAGONS

The two Komodo dragon lizards face-off threateningly, exchanging their lightning-quick and mysterious vocal retorts with forked tongues. They suddenly throw themselves at each other, clashing they rear up on their hind legs and grasp each other in an angry, rough-textured embrace. The struggling pair now stand almost 10 ft (3 m) high. The writhing creatures collapse and the victorious dragon settles one foot on the other dragon's back, confirming its supremacy. The loser staggers away and the victor moves in on its prey, a wounded buffalo. This occurs on Rinca Island in the Komodo archipelago, where we stop for a few weeks. The water is as clear as glass, the coral multi-colored, the beaches pink, and colonies of bats fly out at sunset. The hills and plains are green as far as the eye can see, where deer, buffalo, and monkeys live undisturbed. This is the kingdom of the *Varanus komodoensis*. The only human beings here are the park rangers who periodically patrol the island to keep the paths in order and manage the animals. It was one such of these rangers who came to visit us a week ago to inform us that dragons were attacking a buffalo. Guiding us along a path that is barely visible among the thorny bushes, the ranger explains that the beast had wounded a leg and could not escape. However, he tells us that we don't need to be in a hurry to witness this event because Komodo dragons are lazy and slow predators. After an hour's walk, we finally see the buffalo with a bloody wounded leg at the back end of a marshy clearing, right in the middle of a shallow and muddy pool of water. Around the edges of the water, a dozen dragons have apparently dozed off. Every once in a while, one of the beige animals moves, enters the water and approaches the animal, skimming the buffalo with its slimy tongue, but when the buffalo reacts with its horns the dragon gives up and retreats. This goes on practically all day until the cold-blooded dragons withdraw into the brush at sunset and the buffalo crouches down into the pool of water. We return at dawn, just in time to see the wounded beast suckling its calf that previously fled on still unsure legs when the dragons first began their approach. The dragons besiege the pool of water all day long, attempting sorties

against the buffalo that responds time and again with its horns. This continues until sundown and for the next two days then to a week, the calf fleeing every morning and the buffalo defending itself every day as it becomes progressively more exhausted. Today, however, the beige lizards are more nervous than usual, squabbling and coming to blows. The buffalo now reacts very little and does not even get up from the pool of water. The victorious dragon follows through after the duel, rising up on four thick legs, heading decisively towards the buffalo. The buffalo's horns make an effort at keeping the dragon at bay and the dragon avoids them with an unexpected leap, grasps the buffalo's abdomen in its teeth and pulls. After just one frozen moment, a dozen Komodo dragons attack their prey, which for the first time in one week emits one long, hoarse bellowing moo. Then silence immediately falls over their horrible meal.

174-175 The dragon enters the pool and approaches the buffalo, grazing it, but once the beast reacts with its horns the monitor lizard gives up and retreats.

175 top The Varanus komodoensis is a primitive animal and survives only in the Komodo archipelago because it has no predators or carnivorous competitors here.

175 center Two monitor lizards hurl themselves at each other, clash, rise up on their back feet, and wrap each other in an angry embrace, creating a single,

coarsely-textured entity. After a horrible struggle, the Komodo dragon proves victorious, setting a foot on the back of its rival, thus proclaiming its supremacy.

Komodo

175 bottom Monitor lizards wound their prey in a surprise bite then wait for the bacteria in their mouths to induce infection, causing the beast's eventual death.

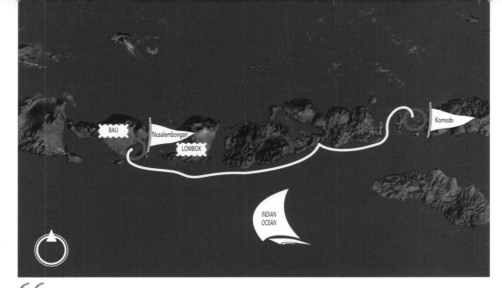

" *250 Miles. Four days along a continuous bridge of islands, arriving at an arid islet where a new and original endeavor is being pursued.* "

Nusalembongan

FARMERS OF THE SEA

A lot of strange tapping noises wake us up. It sounds like beating drums, but as we are anchored in the middle of a bay we don't know what it could be. We get out onto the well deck and a surprising show welcomes us. In the direction of the land, a crowd of people are ambling through the shallow water towing baskets and pushing canoes. There is no artificial light, only the light of the moon and one bright star, but everyone seems to know how to move and where to go. They continue on for a while then gradually move away as the tide rises and then they disappear. All of this occurs within just 150 or so feet (45 m) of our anchorage, on the leeward side of the Nusalembongans islet. We do not dare to go out to watch them in the dark, but we do go on land just after the sun rises. When we come ashore we find dozens of colored "streamers," including greens, browns, yellows, and pinks, scattered throughout the village. We discover that it is seaweed, ramified seaweed, similar to fleshy and pulpy shrubs, separated by color and laid out to dry on plastic sheeting.

We already knew that similar cultivation had been attempted in Indonesia, but we had never witnessed such an impressive show. Inhabitants of Nusalembongans who were once fishermen and salt "salesmen" have transformed themselves into *sea farmers* within just a few years, and the sea around the island reveals incredible stretches of "cultivated fields" beneath the water's surface. As with all farmers worldwide, work and rest beat time to the rhythms of nature. Only at low tide can these "farmers" enter the water, attend to their "fields," clean up their rows of crops, plant new seaweed, and harvest mature algae. It doesn't matter whether they do it in the middle of the night, at dawn, in the rain or on a sunny day. When the tide is low, inhabitants of Nusalembongans pour into the sea. Men, women, and children enter the warm sea and remain literally immersed for hours as they lay out long garlands of seaweed among the submerged rows and insert stakes into the seabed, the very reason for the noise we heard on the first night.

Everyone at Nusalembongans is dedicated to cultivating seaweed, even its senior citizens who, along with the smallest children, go out to glean and harvest every single piece of seaweed that detaches from the crop rows and washes up onto the beach. From the island, this dried seaweed is sent to distant places where carrageenan is extracted, a powdered gelling or solidifying agent that is in very high demand in the industrial world. It is used in the food, pharmaceutical, and cosmetics industries to make sausage, shampoo, lotions, and creams, all very sophisticated products that the inhabitants of Nusalembongans will never see or use. On this arid islet, which once made only a meager living from the salt business and fishing, the arrival of algae has brought unexpected prosperity and represents a balanced use of the natural resources of the sea.

176 bottom Men, women, and children are in the sea for hours laying out and staking very long seaweed garlands along submerged crop rows.

176-177 Once fishermen, the inhabitants of Nusalembongans have now become over the course of just a few years true farmers of the sea.

177 bottom left Brown algae is mature and may be harvested. It is brought to the village to be sorted then laid out to dry.

177 bottom right Ramified seaweed, similar to fleshy and pulpy shrubs, are separated by color and laid out to dry on plastic sheeting throughout the village.

66 *20 Miles. Just five hours through the currents of the Lombok Strait to enter a channel leading into the large natural port of an island permeated with a serene, tolerant, and quiet spirituality.* 99

Bali

SPIRITUALITY AND TOLERANCE

The girl wears yellow fabric around her waist. She bows down before the little altar, refreshing the sticks of incense and offers them up, then sprinkles herself with holy water and leaves. This little ceremony lasts just a few minutes and takes place inside a restaurant among scantily clad tourists, accompanied by the deafening sound of music and car engines outside on the street. The Balinese people are tolerant and their spiritual relationships are so strong and positive that the physical context has no bearing on them. For these people, every place with a religious icon is a temple and at every restaurant, bar, office, and street corner there is just such a symbol.

In Bali, it is impossible not to notice the distinct spirituality that permeates the air. Chaotic traffic suddenly stops for a procession of women in yellow silk sarongs balancing trays on their heads laden with offerings and followed by a line of men playing traditional instruments. Until the last person passes, not one single vehicle dares move. While jumbo jets pass overhead continuously as they come into to land at Denpasar Airport, fishermen cast their nets from small unsteady colored canoes in the port of Benoa, murmuring a prayer. Just a few hundred yards away from buses discharging hordes of tourists, there is always a temple or two where *gamelans* play (traditional instrumental ensemble). One day on the dock, a sign appears: "Today after sunset, preparations for Nyepi, the Hindu New Year, will begin. From midnight tonight to sunset tomorrow, no one will drive in Bali, please do not turn on any lights, or do any cooking. Boat crews are asked not to leave their boats and to limit themselves to work below deck." *Nyepi* ("Day of Silence") is the ceremony of purification of evil spirits. At sunset on the night before, the Balinese people begin to drive away any evil spirits lurking in the city. They do this by striking iron plates and beating on lampposts, drums and cans, anything made of metal within reach. In the *warung* where we have dinner, the chef spends the evening beating pots and pans together, exhorting us to return to our boat on time. As we rush back, we run into groups of kids with torches, traveling the neighborhood to drive out any unwanted spirits. They go from corner to corner, from street to street, not missing a beat in order to chase away any hidden demons with both fire and noise. The coastline is entirely aflame with torches and resounds with noisy activity. Upon returning to the boat, we look around us at the dark bay, as dozens of catamarans cross it with engines running, bringing

178 bottom More than one million tourists come to Bali each year but the Balinese people have not modified their way of life, traditions, or spirituality despite any perceived outside influence.

178-179 The shape of this craft retains its ancient, characteristic, and traditional form, the sail is fabricated with recycled fabric, but these boats still hold up well at sea.

179 bottom Along the coast, the fishermen's old wooden canoes of green, blue, and yellow coexist with the luxury motorized craft that tourists take out for a cruise.

tourists back from sunset cruises. The street is an infinite line of car and moped headlights while planes landing or taking off pass overhead every 15 minutes. It is difficult to believe that everything will actually stop for 24 hours. But stop it does. The next day, not one boat moves in the port, not even one canoe is paddled. The island's main street is deserted, we only count three planes throughout the whole day, and don't even see one trail of smoke rising from a chimney. We hear only the strident calls of birds, clanking noises of halyards against flag posts, palm fronds moving in the wind, and the swishing sounds of the sea. Evil spirits may return to the island, but on seeing no signs of life they believe it to be uninhabited and abandon it once again.

180-181 and 181 top As part of the numerous religious ceremonies characterizing the lives of the Balinese people, these women balance trays on their heads laden with fruit and other foods to offer at the temple.

181 center Cockfights, although bloody, form part of the island's way of life. Champion cocks are fed, coddled, and trained on a daily basis.

181 bottom To the Balinese, every place with a religious symbol is a temple and there is just such an icon in every restaurant, bar, office, and on every street corner.

Bali

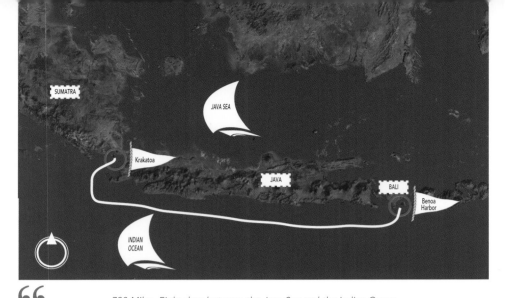

" *730 Miles. Eight days between the Java Sea and the Indian Ocean to arrive next at an island created only 100 years ago, the product of the largest volcanic explosion in the recorded history of the planet.* "

Krakatoa

THE VOLCANO'S SON

On 26 August, 1883, the volcano on the island of Krakatoa literally exploded, ejecting a column of fire and detritus almost 12.5 miles (20 km) high. For three days the island remained enveloped in flames and black clouds, and when these had dissipated more than two-thirds of Krakatoa had disappeared. But that was just the beginning! That apocalyptic explosion had actually created an abyss under the volcano, and the island remained suspended without foundations until dawn the next day when it finally collapsed. What remained of the island sank, creating a chasm that pulled the surrounding sea down into it. Entering the fissure, the water came into contact with the hot lava and suddenly transformed into an superheated ball of vapor that caused another very violent explosion, forming a column 262,000 ft (80,000 m) in height over the crater (ten times the height of Mount Everest)! A horrible roar was heard more than 3,100 miles (5,000 km) away, the wave of pressure generated by the explosion created recurring tremors through the ground, while the sea first receded from nearby coasts then formed a tsunami that spread in every direction, swelling and increasing in height as the water's depth decreased. A tsunami of almost 100 ft (30 m) crashed into Java and Sumatra, destroying everything in its path. Almost 5 cubic miles (20 cubic km) of white-hot material was ejected and deposited in the sea, creating a layer of pumice up to 10 ft (3 m) floating on the water. Some 40,000 people were killed and this devastating event crippled the region for years.

In 1928, near what remained of Krakatoa, yet another eruption occurred, this time underwater, forming the new island of *Anak* Krakatoa, the "son" of Krakatoa, which has grown steadily since that time. When we disembark on the hot, black-sand beach of Anak Krakatoa, the young island "son" is already more than 70 years old and stands out against the sky more than 650 ft (200 m) above sea level. We clamber up what have become the slopes of a volcano covered with yellowish foul-smelling slicks. A puff of steam comes out of each and every rock formation, while the air is heavy with smoke, heat, and humidity. We seem to be in a pressure cooker. Every few steps, we turn around to look down at our boat, perhaps anchored too close to the shore on the unstable and steep seabeds just off the island. We go up further still but the terrain under our feet feels progressively hotter and, despite shoes and socks, it is uncomfortable to proceed, even breathing becomes difficult because of the heat and smell of sulfur. We climb up as far as we dare and quickly take some photos before descending. We move down as rapidly as we can, while all around us we hear a constant rumbling from the depths as if the volcano's "son" beneath us is protesting our presence. Yet, in the midst of this Dante-esque scene there is plenty of life – tiny butterflies, crickets, beetles, praying mantises, flies, and gnats. Further below, the basin of a small valley is sprinkled with small plants, ferny bushes, and violet flowers that have appeared seemingly from nowhere and are growing in nonexistent soil. Seeds and the insects were transported here by the wind or birds and now they are colonizing, cultivating, and refining this barren, blasted realm.

182-183 and 183 bottom On 26 August, 1883 a fiery column of detritus almost 12.5 miles (20 km) high burst out of the volcano on the island of Krakatoa and for three years the island was enveloped in black clouds. Krakatoa ejected almost 5 cubic miles (20 cubic km) of material into the sea, creating a 10-ft (3-m) thick layer of pumice on the water. In 1928, near what remained of Krakatoa, an eruption on the seabed occurred and the result was Anak Krakatoa, the son of Krakatoa.

184-185 and 185 bottom
Borneo is the third largest island
in the world, and consists of
Kalimantan (Indonesia), Sarawak
(Malaysia), and the small
sultanate of Brunei.

184 bottom The Green Boat is
anchored here in a sheltered
finger of the sea, leeward of an
uninhabited islet 20 miles (32 km)
off the coast of Borneo.

186-187 When the sky is
overcast, the sun sometimes
bursts through a gap in the
clouds, illuminating lower clouds
with incredible tones of pink and
orange.

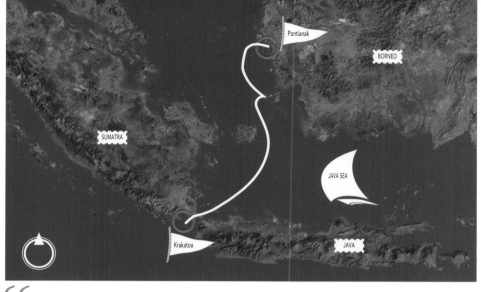

*520 Miles. Five days through the Java Sea from Sumatra to Borneo,
two of the largest islands in the world.*

Borneo

A RIVER THROUGH THE FOG

Smoke in the open sea surprises us. Its odor is carried on a slight, warm breeze, the same breeze that allowed us to slip silently into the darkness of the night. The sea is calm but that odor is everywhere. We study everything around us to locate its source but can't see a thing, just a sort of light fog that blurs the brilliance of the stars. At five a.m. a bit of light finally comes through, but a cocoon-like atmosphere obscures the morning sun like an autumn fog. The haze prevents us from seeing anything and we have to trust our instruments to sail on. GPS tracking points us straight at the estuary of the Kapuas, the longest river in Borneo. The river port of Pontianak is where we are headed and this is just a few miles upstream from there. At 10 a.m. according to our instruments, we should be in the middle of the estuary at the point where the map marks the beginning of the entrance canal, but the fog doesn't lift, not even a buoy appears, and the water depth descends to below 16 ft (5 m). The odor is more intense than before and we continue to advance blindly towards a land that persists in not revealing itself.

When we are about to give up, we sight a *phinisi*, a traditional Indonesian transport boat sailing in the same direction as we are. We follow it like a beacon until Pontianak appears within the fog. It is a big city of streets, markets, and other storefront businesses. The river cuts it in half and is its umbilical cord connecting it to the world. Cargo ships leave from the river headed towards the rest of Indonesia and the smallest boats may go upstream along the river for hundreds of miles into the heart of Borneo. Along the wooden wharves, there are barges unloading goods, warehouses, sawmills, simple little houses on piles, and hundreds of fishing boats crowding the pier adjacent to an enormous floating market. It is a bustling place teeming with people and things, completely enshrouded in a blanket of smog. And it's always like this! It is a phenomenon that occurs as a result of a process that has been repeated over the years. To prepare the fields for new crops, farmers set fire to them, the fire often spreads to the forest and even further. Over the years the situation has worsened and caused serious deforestation.

When Borneo was once covered by primary forest, the jungle was extremely dense and humid, and any fires burned out on their own. Today, the territory is covered by open secondary forest and savannah that burns far more easily. Fires spread over hundreds of square miles in an immense territory where no one can control them. Transported by the trade wind, the smoke from all of these fires moves leeward of the island, exactly where we are now. In some years, the smoke was so intense that it traveled all the way to Malaysia, into the Malacca Canal, and even the Singapore airport had to close due to fog. In one month at Pontianak, we never see the sun. Inevitably, the white in our flag yellows as does the sail cover. Everything smells like smoke on the boat, the sheets, our clothes, and even our bread. However, the people that live on the wharves and in the pile dwellings along the river don't seem to mind or make a big deal out of it. Should we?

185

Borneo

188 Rivers that flow through inland cities and villages are the umbilical cords that connect them to the rest of the world.

188-189 The smallest boats may go upstream along the tributaries of the river for hundreds of miles towards the heart of Borneo.

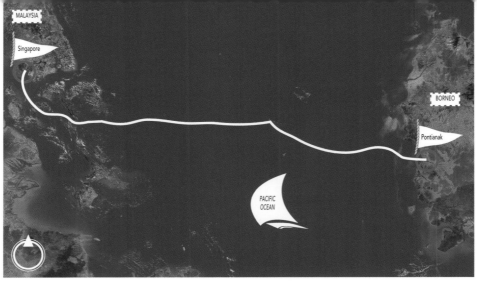

" 380 Miles. Five days across the South China Sea, arriving
in one of the largest ports in the world. "

Singapore
IS THIS OUR FUTURE?

It takes an eternity to cross the port of Singapore. We have never seen so many large ships and so many different types, not even at the entrance to the Panama Canal. We sail for miles through the chaos of towers, cranes, silos, buoys, and various traffic signals and signs. We take a slalom course between enormous drilling platforms, refineries that look like cathedrals, gigantic floating dock facilities that upon seeing their open and empty interiors seem to be the size of ten football fields. We very quickly pass hundreds of little lighters, all the while risking the unintentional capsize of one of the dilapidated little Indonesian boats full of bananas, coconuts, and other produce. The people in them are indifferent to all the hectic activity of the port and still greet us with an easy sense of humor. The sea at Singapore is grey,

dirty, and rough, as if a storm had just passed through and yet there is no wind. The reason for these swells is just an overabundance of propellers in such a relatively confined area. The air is heavy with heat and smoke, and the city's skyscrapers are our constant backdrop view, providing only a glimpse of the hills beyond. We are dazed, tired, and distressed. All these days of sailing, all this hard work, and all this stress just to reach this destination, this horrible place?! The bedlam around us is so colorless, so dirty, and so hyper-industrialized that it seems surreal. Then suddenly, the old signal mast appears. It is actually the wooden mast from a sailing ship, erected on the hills and held in place with lots of stays and crosstrees, and was once used to raise signal flags and give ships maneuvering instructions, including the current flow rate and direction, anchorage locations, the presence of relative authorities in the city, and whatever other information might be required by mariners. Its old flag, strung up on the hills long ago, is still there, waving up above the cranes and silos, an old relic in this world of glass and concrete. We disembark and everything transforms. The streets are orderly and very clean with numerous skyscrapers, sparkling shop windows, buses coming and going on a precise timetable, subway stations finished in polished marble, beautiful and expensive hotels, as well as streams of well-mannered and well-dressed people. Is this our future? Will our grandchildren live in this aseptic neat and tidy post-industrial environment? What happened to the ancient ways of Asian culture? We find a faint memory of that age in the large food stalls located in the commercial centers, where, despite the habitual order and cleanliness, they haven't yet found a way to diminish the odors of garlic and curry, thus wrapping the surroundings in a cloud redolent of those ancient times.

190 bottom It takes an eternity to cross the port of Singapore, navigating for hours among ships of every kind and size, small boats, signaling devices, buoys, and small lighters along the way.

191 The sea water outside Singapore is turbulent as if a storm has just passed, but there is no wind and the reason for these swells is just that there are too many propellers operating in the water.

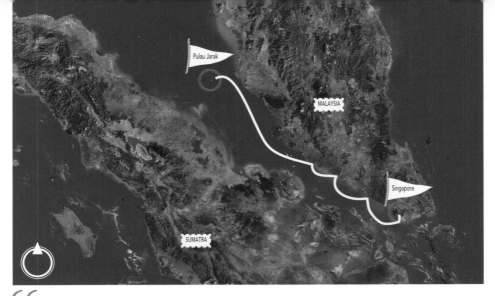

" 270 Miles. Five days. The narrow Strait of Malacca between the coast of Malaysia and the island of Sumatra, through which most of the world's merchant shipping passes, owes its infamous reputation to acts of piracy. "

The Strait of Malacca

THE MEMORY OF PIRATES

Looking at its 400 miles (640 km) of shallow water on the map, the first impression of the Strait of Malacca is that it is a fascinating place, where over the centuries countless Arab *feluccas*, Portuguese *caraccas*, Dutch merchant ships, and English clippers have passed through. All were going to the East loaded with goods and only sometimes successfully returning to the West with holds full of cloves, nutmeg, and cinnamon. Today, a half of the world's maritime traffic sails through this strait, passing Malaysia, Indonesia, and Singapore. But it is a dangerous place. Its muddy waters have infamous, violent currents and there are other threats. "Be careful, there are pirates in that strait," the usually well informed say. "No, they are just a myth, pirates haven't traveled that strait for years," others reassure. "Yes, a few things have happened here, but pirates just attack large ships," the Malaysian authorities admit. We are here sailing through the strait along the Malaysian coast, unsure whether we can expect to have any strange encounters. Our video cameras are ready to capture whatever occurs. But what will happen? Will there be boats full of shady-looking people? Skirmishes in the midst of the water? Or ships using

fire hydrants to drive away attacking pirates? In fact, there is just an incredible amount of traffic, including ships, fishing boats without any signal lights, and even poles driven into the seabed that seem to have been put there just to make the careless run aground. During the powerful gusts of a storm, a loud resounding noise informs us that something on the boat has broken. The boat no longer responds to controls and the tiller turns freely as if the rudder blade is no longer there, while the sails flap furiously and the hull continues to rotate uncontrollably. Around us a dozen ships and fishing boats appear and disappear in the violent rain being emptied from lowering black clouds. We send out a radio communication to let people know that we aren't able to maneuver and run to the locker for emergency spare parts, searching for the steering shaft, head, a bolt, and a wrench to stop the free-moving tiller. The rain is pouring down and the close proximity of the horns on ships skimming past are giving us goose pimples, but in just ten minutes the emergency tiller tightens down. It is hard to maneuver but the situation is under control, we are holding our own in the storm, able to avoid other ships, and start devising a solution. We need to stop and repair the rudder but where? The traffic to the east along the Malaysian coast is imposing. The Indonesian coast is far away and to reach it we would have to sail throughout the night. Then, a surprise! We discover on the chart that the very small islet of Pulau Jarak is only 10 miles (16 km) away. We head there, exploiting the last of the storm's wind gusts, and after not even two hours the rays from the setting sun illuminate the silhouette of a tiny uninhabited island, barely half a square mile and covered in virgin forest. We anchor, replacing broken lines and everything is back in working order. The next morning we make another discovery. The water beneath the keel is transparent and at just 25 miles (40 km) further off the coast, the sea water transforms from the most contaminated on the planet to the cleanest and clearest. There are banks of thriving coral, gigantic moray eels, and thousands of colorful fish, not suffering a hint of pollution.

192 bottom Rivers pouring into the sea carry whatever they encounter along the way downstream. This large tree trunk could also be a potential danger.

192-193 After barely two hours, the rays of the setting sun illuminate the silhouette of a tiny, uninhabited island covered in virgin forest. It is Pulau Jarak.

193 bottom Langkawi archipelago's small, island administrative seat in Malaysian territory is covered with primary forest and is a highly popular local tourist destination.

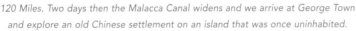

" *120 Miles. Two days then the Malacca Canal widens and we arrive at George Town and explore an old Chinese settlement on an island that was once uninhabited.* "

George Town

A NEIGHBORHOOD OF PILE DWELLINGS

The Penang coastline changes shape at low tide. Rocks appear at the surface in some places, at others the roots of mangrove trees are exposed, some of the beaches double their width, while another area is riddled with muddy marshland. Two centuries ago, the Chinese built a village on piles facing this marshland. It was their idea to settle in a place that was protected by the jungle and its creatures and also where the sea converged with the land daily, so naturally cleaning up the refuse produced by human habitation. With the passage of years, the jungle has disappeared and been replaced by the burgeoning Malaysian city of George Town, the Chinese quarter still remains a small city unto itself, just a hop, skip, and a jump over the sea. Like all the nearby cities, it has a port and those who arrive here from the mainland must pass under wooden arches in the shape of 13-ft (4-m) tall dragons – the always alert sentinels.

Arriving by sea, we have to anchor a long way from the shore because the seabed is soft and shallow. In order to disembark we must use the small sampan service that circulates continuously throughout the port, ready to quickly respond to calls from anyone who wants to get to the land. Only these sampan sailors know where to land, avoiding the black viscous and muddy areas that shift according to the tide. Our Charon is a very stocky Chinese man who looks like Buddha incarnate. He transports us without a word, drops us off near a small temple at the end of a long wooden jetty and only when we give him the two *ringits* required does he smile and bestow upon us a kind of blessing.

Dwellings are lined up along the sides of the jetty, each one with a veranda and small gate that lead inside the house. There are other jetties parallel to us, all connected by wooden footbridges. This city has an ancient rhythm, a great sense of humanity, and many fascinating sights. There are old and wrinkled senior citizens who spend their time with legs crossed on the beams of verandas sorting grains of rice, selecting soybean shoots, boning chicken, and completing the other ordinary tasks that contribute to the daily routine of life. A fisherman, heedless of the filth floating in the water, casts out his net from the veranda of his home. A family of artisans craft statues of the Buddha for the forthcoming Chinese New Year, endowing the gooey gesso with a likeness born from wisdom. A tiny boy with shiny black hair sculpted down over his forehead enjoys his soup, where small pieces of vegetables and scraps of egg float, and alternately uses a ceramic spoon and wooden chopsticks.

We are here at *durian* season and each morning a boy with a handcart full of this extremely popular fruit passes over the jetties. They give off a very strong acidic and pungent odor, so much so that the inhabitants of this Chinese pile-dwelling neighborhood keep them outside on their verandas. However, to them the *durian* is the most succulent fruit in the world and they anxiously await the time when it is in season. The nauseating smell coming from every veranda accompanies us all the way to the dragon arches. Quickly thereafter we again encounter the city with its cacophony of sounds and the odor of the *durian* fruit is lost and replaced by that of traffic fumes.

194 bottom At low tide, the coast of Penang changes and along some stretches, rocks are exposed while at others, the roots of mangroves are revealed and a muddy marshland suddenly appears.

194-195 Two centuries ago, the Chinese constructed a village of pile dwellings overlooking marshland in order to settle in a place protected from the jungle and its animal inhabitants.

195 bottom Dwellings with verandas line the sides of the jetty with other jetties parallel to this one, all connected by wooden footbridges.

196-197 and 196 bottom left *New Panganga Bay is immense and sprinkled with sheer-sided islets with steep peaks that transform it into a labyrinth with unexplored grottos.*

196 bottom right *Towards sunset when tourist boats return home the fishermen's launches go out and set their traps. Fishing is the main activity in this area.*

197 bottom *As you navigate north, the bay gradually narrows and the water turns greener and more opaque from a low turnover rate and increase in temperature.*

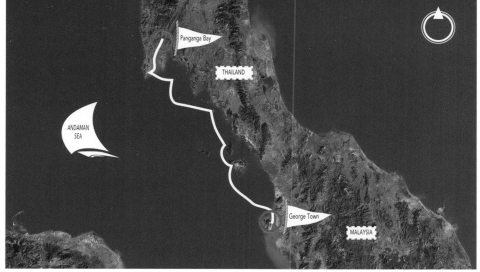

> *120 Miles. Three days to get to a large narrow bay between the coast of Thailand and the island of Phuket.*

Panganga Bay

AN ENCHANTING LOCALE

There is a bay between Phuket Island and the coast of Thailand that gradually narrows as you navigate north. It is called Panganga Bay and it is immense, uninhabited, silent, and sprinkled with an intricate and bewildering maze of islets with steep peaks rising sheer from the sea, many with secret tunnels and unexplored caves. We sail for days in complete solitude through this extraordinary landscape until one day we encounter canoes. They are speedy, wooden, tapered launches equipped with outboard motors and very long driveshafts. They appear and disappear amongst the maze of islets and just when the roar of one engine fades, the echo of the next one bounces off the rock walls surrounding us. There is a man and a woman in each boat, the woman stands at the prow with an almost 7-ft (2-m) long stick in her hand, while the man is in the stern, operating the motor. Every now and again, the woman dips the stick into the water and scoops something up. Out of curiosity, we approach in our dinghy. With nets attached to the ends of their sticks, the women catch enormous jellyfish of almost 2 ft (60 cm) in diameter. Each time a woman locates a jellyfish, she gives directions to her partner, waiting until they are right over it, drops her net, traps it, and dumps it in the middle of the canoe, all the while balancing on the canoe bottom covered with a slimy mucus-type substance left by the jellyfish.

Jellyfish catching continues for the whole morning until the overloaded canoes head back towards the coast. We follow them and land on a small beach where about 20 boats are lined up. Indifferent to the nauseating smell that permeates the area, fishermen unload their catch with bear hands, piling the jellyfish into large baskets that they transport off the beach to a clearing where collection tubs await them. The flabby jellyfish land in the tubs with a thud then the women sprinkle them with salt and cover them with lengths of cloth. The dense and transparent mucus-like substance dripping from the baskets makes everything slimy, including the canoes, the fishermen's clothing, arms, legs, and

heads. It looks like a reenactment of something written by Dante! After filling the first tub of jellyfish, they continue with others as a dozen or so women take care of moving their catch from the baskets to the tubs and preserving them with salt. It is 100 degrees outside and the terrible stench remains suspended in the thick and heavy air.

They explain to us that their village depends mainly on catching cuttlefish and calamari for the majority of the year. However, jellyfish come here to reproduce during this season, so the villagers stop whatever else they are doing and dedicate themselves to this strange fishing technique for just a few days. However, the boats are still in service for several weeks for delivery to market. Once salted, jellyfish bodies lose water and take on more consistency day after day. Finally, they complete their transformation into rubbery and tough yellowish disks similar to pork rinds, worth 12 dollars per kilo (2.2 lb), and are much sought-after delicacies to the Chinese. We wait in terror for the moment when we will have to try this delicacy, but they reassure us by saying: "In China, everyone eats jellyfish but here, we are too familiar with their stench to ever have the slightest desire to even taste them!"

198-199 The Moken people move continuously between Burma, Thailand, and Malaysia, following the monsoons, the ancient rhythms and calls of the sea.

198 bottom Their village consists of about 20 pile dwellings built at one end of the beach. It is a magnificent place with very clean water and sheltered from the wind.

199 bottom Formerly pirates, they would suddenly appear in flotillas of small boats, surround their victim, climb aboard, empty the ship, and disappear.

" *160 Miles. After several days of searching, we happen upon the last refuge of an ancient people.* "

Surin Islands

NOMADS OF THE SEA

The chief wears a tattered shirt, threadbare shorts, and has an intelligent face. When we point to our boat he makes a yes sign and smiles. When we tell him we are from Italy he doesn't understand. To him, Italy means nothing. There are about 120 people in the village, the last surviving community of a once numerous people. They have dark complexions and are small with almost Mongolian features and not at all like the Malaysians or the Thai people, even though they have shared the coasts of the Malacca Strait with them for centuries, moving constantly between Burma, Thailand, and Malaysia. They are called the Moken, living a large part of the year in long shallow boats built of wood curved through the application of heat and blackened by many layers of shark's liver fat. They can cook, eat, sleep, and above all move from place to place in their boats continuously, following the monsoons, fish, and sea turtles. They live according to the ancient rhythms and calls of the sea that only they can recognize. We had talked about them quite a bit but in vague terms as people would speak of things with which they have no direct experience. After searching for them for weeks, we find them in the Surin Islands, 80 miles (130 km) off the coast of Thailand, on a distant island well away from the most well-traveled routes.

Their village consists of about 20 pile or stilt dwellings built at the one end of the beach. It is a magnificent place situated by a sort of channel between two islands, sheltered from the wind and with very clean water. The nomads of the sea survive on whatever they can catch: fish, shellfish, and sea turtles, supplementing their seafood diet with wild tubers found in the forest when they stopover for a time on dry land. At one time, they were also pirates. During periods of high winds when the monsoon and the sea made it difficult for ship crews to sail, the Moken would suddenly appear out of the maze of islands along the coast. In flotillas of 10 to 20 boats they would surround their victim, go on board ship,

kill everyone, empty the ship, and then vanish among the reefs.

It is difficult to associate this sort of savagery with the kind and intelligent eyes of their chief. It is increasingly harder to believe when looking at the youngsters in the village, peacefully intent upon constructing a canoe, or when observing the women stretched out on the sand, calm and indifferent. The chief says that they have neither a school nor teachers, neither doctors nor medicine, that they really have nothing. Yet, seeing them dive in more than 30 ft (9 m) of water to fish without masks or oxygen tanks, watching them sail at night among the reefs without any maps, compasses, or nautical instruments, we realize that they have something that we know nothing about: complete communion with the sea.

Surin Islands

200 top The Moken live a large part of the year in wooden boats where they cook, eat, and sleep, but in the slack period between the two monsoons, they stopover on land.

200 bottom These nomads of the sea survive on what they're able to catch, including fish, shellfish, sea turtles, and wild tubers they find in the forest when they stopover on dry land.

201 The Moken are not citizens of any particular country and often encounter opposition from government officials stopping along the coasts in the slack periods between one monsoon and the next.

202-203 *The Mahatma Gandhi Marine National Park, 15 miles (24 km) south of Port Blair, was created to protect these natural environments.*

202 bottom *The Indian colonists of these extraordinary islands have brought their own traditions with them, including fishing with drop-nets.*

203 bottom *For every stopover within the archipelago, you must request permission from the port authority and contact them by radio once arriving at your destination.*

204-205 *The sea and its tidal range shapes massive rock formations, eroding them and thus creating islets in the form of gigantic mushrooms.*

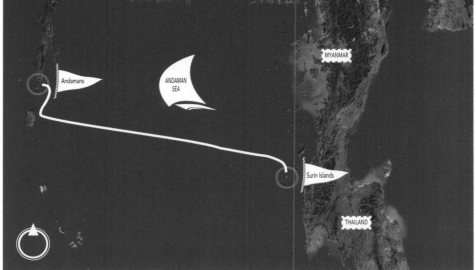

" *350 Miles. Four days and we arrive at an archipelago that has only been accessible for just a few years, sheltering the last people of the Negritos tribe.* "

The Andamans

ISLANDS OF THE NEGRITOS

Two centuries ago, the Andamans were just islands lost in the middle of the sea, covered in forest, rich in fresh water, and as yet uninhabited. At least that is what the British thought when they came from India looking for a distant land where they could transport hundreds of Indian political prisoners. Those prisoners were neither criminals nor thieves so they couldn't incarcerate them for long periods of time, making martyrs out of them, but they couldn't set them free either. Deportation to the Andamans seemed a good solution. Thus, the British founded the city of Port Blair, built a prison camp, and sent there all those they considered politically undesirable. A century later, India gained its independence, the deportees became heroes, the prison camp was closed, and everyone was free to return to their homes. However, many of those people decided to remain and formed the nucleus of the Indian colonies that remain on the Andamans to this day.

The British were wrong in thinking that these islands were uninhabited, however, because the Negritos people lived and still do live there! They were a small population, divided into just a few tribes of several hundred people, hidden in the forest, intentionally not wearing any clothes, not cultivating anything, living off on fruit and roots. They didn't use any metal implements and were not even familiar with the technique for making fire and so would leave any naturally igniting fire to burn. They had only spears, bows and arrows, and were very skilled at using them for hunting wild pigs and fish. In almost total isolation, the Negritos remained as they were until India became independent. They then had their first contact with newcomers, which, though sporadic, brought disease and cultural disorientation. The Onge tribe who allowed closer contact with the Indians, accepting donations of food, clothing, and other items, lost their ability to hunt and

survive in the forest in just a few years. Another tribe, the Jarawa, hid in the forests north of Port Blair and only rarely had contact with government officials who tried to monitor them. However, on the island of Sentinel, just 20 miles (32 km) from Port Blair, a totally untouched tribe took shelter. They were and still are a group of people that live in the Stone Age, the only example of such a society still existing on Earth. The people of Sentinel are not familiar with the use of iron, do not farm, and do not know how to make a fire. Paradoxically, however, they are familiar with the planes that fly over the Gulf of Bengal and among their primitive implements there are certainly some made from pieces of plastic that wash up on shore. The Sentinel people still greet anyone who comes ashore on their island with poisonous arrows and the Indian authorities have decided to leave them undisturbed for now.

We pass by the coast of Sentinel and look at it from a distance through binoculars. All we see is an empty beach and a lot of forest. We imagine its inhabitants, hiding who knows where, watching our sailboat. We are not at all positive that we should attempt to violate their precious isolation.

206-207 and 206 bottom left
Although an outboard motor has
now been added to the transom,
the fishermen's boats are still the
old outrigger canoes.

206 bottom right The land of
milk and honey was what people
once called this lush green island
rich in fresh water, precious
gems, and ancient cultures.

207 bottom In the port at Galle,
sheltered from the sea and wind,
sailboats are the only craft to
take refuge, stopping over after
crossing the Indian Ocean.

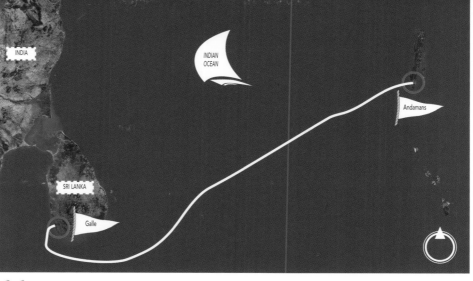

" *850 Miles. Nine days to cross only half the Bay of Bengal. Arriving here in a boat adds a dash of adventure.* "

Galle

A BUOY WITH A BELL

The marina at Galle at the southwestern end of Sri Lanka is a well-protected area, sheltered from the sea and wind. In this marina, sailboats take refuge during their crossings of the Indian Ocean, making a stopover at this island once described as the land of milk and honey. There is a large buoy with a bell anchored just off the marina. The buoy moves back and forth with every wave and the bell rings. It is the only buoy with a bell that we've ever seen in our years of sailing. Its purpose is to send out a sound signal rather than a visual one, but the sad and raucous metallic sound it emits is not what you would expect and gives the impression of some dark danger lurking, such as in the past when an epidemic was indicated with a yellow flag and a ringing bell.

It is the middle of the night when we arrive in the vicinity of the buoy. In the distant marina we catch a glimpse of lights and masts of boats anchored there. We are tired because sailing from the Andamans took longer than expected due to changes in the temperamental monsoon that after 12 hours completely abandoned us, slowing us down even further. We have detailed maps and precise directions to the channel that leads to the marina and would have attempted to get there anyway despite the late hour, attracted by the prospect of spending an entire night on an anchored boat. We are about to do just that when a more deafening bell ring surprises us. We decide to let it go and remain faithful to a resolution we made years ago: never enter a port at night. We lower almost all of the sails and put on the sail cover so that the boat will stop. We alternate, one sleeping and the other on deck, to keep watch for anything that might collide with us during the night. The southern tip of Sri Lanka itself is like a buoy placed in the midst of the ocean and it has to be passed

by all of the ships going from Asia to Europe and vice versa.

Dawn finally comes and illuminates the grayish water. We can see the land and the line of dilapidated buoys leading in the direction of the port. We reach the port in just half an hour and slow down because the entrance is tiny, then we notice a boat moving from one breakwater towards the end of the opposite breakwater. A dozen men on the boat are rolling an enormous net around a pole. At first we think they are fishermen but then we see their military uniforms and observe that the mesh in the net is made of iron. Later, they explain to us that it is an anti-terrorist net and that every evening they cast it out as a barrier to prevent anyone from entering the port during the night. If it weren't for the dismal ringing of the bell, we would have found ourselves stuck in the net and in who knows what other kind of bureaucratic mess.

208-209 Perched on wooden poles in the sea halfway between the water's edge and the line of breakers, the men of Galle fish using the most traditional of methods.

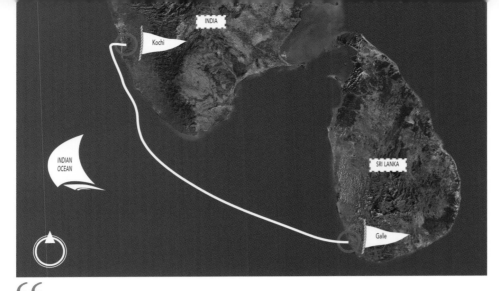

400 Miles. Five days. The last 100 miles (160 km) along the coast of India requires concentration sailing through an incredible amount of traffic with small fishing boats remarkable distances from land.

Kochi

IMMERSED IN THE PAST

We spend the whole night sailing with very little wind, surrounded by worrisome silent and almost invisible presences on the calm, dark, and moonless sea. We intuitively sense the nearness of someone only due to the reddish phantom of a small brazier in the bottom of their boat's hull, while we would not have noticed others if it weren't for their whispering occupants who perceive our close proximity when they are just a few yards away and collision seems inevitable. These invisible sailors, not used to encountering sailboats, approach our boat lights to see us up close, forcing us to constantly do emergency maneuvers in order to avoid potentially disastrous contact with them. At dawn all of these boats slide along with us into the funnel

of a narrow and tricky channel that leads into the enormous lagoon of Kochi. They are small patched-up boats with shabby hulls and most of them less than 25 ft (8 m) in length. They are equipped with tattered sails and repaired oars. Although they are small, there are many of them and in this barely 100-ft (30-m) wide channel a certain amount of concentration is needed to avoid them and for them to avoid us! When the channel widens it opens onto an area of protected waterways, which branch off in all directions and that over the centuries have promoted trade and commerce. The ancient city of Kochi was where the first European colonial settlement in India was established in the 16th century by the Portugeuse at Fort Kochi. The Portuguese were followed by the Dutch and then the British, but before the Europeans the Arabs and Chinese had been trading here for a long time and were both anxious to take control of this strategic natural port and its profitable spice trade. Every corner of the old city recalls those who have passed through over the centuries: the churches with white bell towers, the mosques, the old synagogue tiled in white and blue as well as the men's beards and skull caps, the women's black veils and colored saris, the diverse and intense scents of every sort of ethnic cuisine. On the narrow streets, carts pulled by mules, wheelbarrows pushed by semi-naked men, and small three-wheeled vehicles chug along. When the monsoon is in full force in the surrounding hills, the perfume from cardamom plantations permeates the air while dried fish, curry, and piles of peppers in sacks at the shops around the market release a bouquet of daily aromas. We anchor facing an old colonial building with its façade of light-colored, flaking wood and we find ourselves again at a frantic aquatic crossroads. The traffic on the lagoon around us never stops. We see small canoes of fishermen, large barges full of sulfur, motorboats acting as public transportation, small boats with a single oarsman offering anything from ice to pineapples, from fish to coconuts. At sunset, bells ring and we hear the call of the muezzin, see fires sparkling and smoke dancing, sensing the appeals, dirges, and prayers. We feel shrouded by the past and enfolded in history itself.

210 bottom The first to arrive at Kochi were the Arabs and Chinese, then came the Portuguese, Dutch, and finally the English, all searching for a strategic base to establish trading posts.

210-211 At the mouth of the port's channel, the enormous lift nets lower and rise constantly, revealing their catch in flashes of flip-flopping silver.

211 bottom left Despite their small size, there are numerous boats returning at dawn through the narrow, 100-ft (30-m) wide channel, which requires careful and constant attention to avoid collisions.

211 bottom right The waters and seabeds along the coast of India are still rich in fish because fishermen here almost exclusively employ traditional methods.

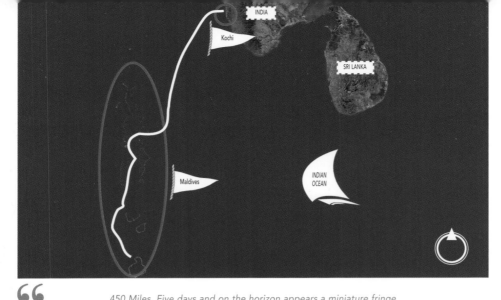

" 450 Miles. Five days and on the horizon appears a miniature fringe
that is actually made up of the trunks of palm trees,
which are sighted first because of the very low-lying atoll. "

The Maldives

FISHING FOR TUNA

Salem is the commander, Ali is second-in-command, and then there are Hussein, Ibrahim, and a mute boy who communicates through unintelligible muttering. Their boat is a *dhoni*, a hull with a slender curved prow and stern on which the Maldivians float over the tepid waters of the most beautiful atolls on the planet. However, these dreamlike atolls and incredible coral banks that attract tourists from all over the world are to the Maldivians just the daily backdrop for a simple and harmonious life, and the azure waters and multi-colored seabeds are only seen as an inexhaustible source of food.

We leave when the sky is still black with just a hint of light in the east. The *dhoni* is not quite 50 ft (15 m) long and just over 13 ft (4 m) wide, with decking only around the sides and an open, empty hold. We will be filling the hold with tuna if the fishing is good. We sail inside the atoll with fishermen that instinctively find their way into the midst of a reef and dangerous shallows. Approaching a coral shelf in the middle of nowhere, we suddenly drop anchor. Two of us dive in while the others lower a net and arrange it horizontally at just a few

yards depth. After a few minutes, those in the water turn and swim with strange movements as if they are dancing. They are closely following a cloud of small fish, pushing and guiding them until they are directly over the net. At that point, we haul up the net and the small live fish end up in the hold, which floods with seawater. This operation is repeated several times and, in just a short while, the belly of the *dhoni* is flashing with silver. We start sailing again, leave the atoll, and begin to patrol the ocean, rising and falling on the gray waves in search of tuna. In order to find them, the fishermen scrutinize the sky, watching for birds signaling schools of fish. Suddenly, the mute boy gesticulates and mumbles, pointing in the distance. Birds!

We approach and below the birds the water seethes with jumping and diving fish, and while one of the fishermen begins to throw in handfuls of live bait, the others frantically prepare their fishing rods and hooks. In a second the water is full of the flip-flopping of little fish and the tuna hurl themselves at them by the hundreds, jumping up from the water all around us. They throw themselves on the little fish, against the hooks, and whatever else is in the water. The fishing rods rise and fall and each time a tuna falls on board, leaping up desperately from the belly of the *dhoni*. The crew free the fish from the hooks, recast their rods, and quickly catch another then another as in the dreams of all fishermen. They fish continuously until the tuna and other fish all mysteriously disappear as in response to a sudden signal. The fishermen are finished.

In a quarter of an hour they have caught about 100 tuna, and so instead of returning to Tulusdoo, the island from where we came, we head towards Malé, the capital, to take the fish to market. It takes some time because Malé is 30 miles (48 km) away, and even though the *dhoni* is speedy we will arrive as it gets dark. The stars, the moon, and the fishermen's great experience will show us the way.

The Maldives

214 and 215 right The dhoni, traditional boats of the Maldives with an arched stern like those of the Viking ships, are used for fishing and transportation.

215 left Tuna is not just the primary food source for the inhabitants of the Maldives, it is also, along with tourism, one of the mainstays of the country's economy.

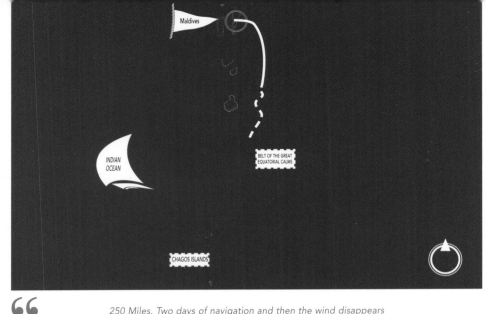

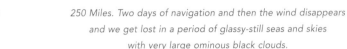

*250 Miles. Two days of navigation and then the wind disappears
and we get lost in a period of glassy-still seas and skies
with very large ominous black clouds.*

The Great Equatorial Calms
EVERYTHING SUDDENLY STOPS

Straddling the equator, there is a zone that marks the boundary between the winds of the northern hemisphere and those of the southern hemisphere. This equatorial region of calms, light winds, and unpredictable storms is also known as the doldrums. It is impossible to anticipate the scale of this largely idle world made up of silence, debilitating stillness, and sudden storms, because its range and position change over the months and with the seasons. Sailors at one time feared the calm more than the storms. Mariners could remain trapped

for months, immobile on the water with sails flapping and rigging dangling, frozen in a kind of windless and timeless spell. Ships' hulls became encrusted with very long seaweed, crews withered in the heat and became ill, food and water were rationed, and with the passage of days the fear of being the victim of a spell took root. With the streamlined profiles of modern sailboats today, a crossing that could once take months can be achieved in one or two weeks. But the region of the calms still remains a difficult and perplexing challenge, whether for the boat or those on board.

We leave Malé with a wind that pushes us cheerfully southward. After 48 hours at 2° north, the wind calms down and everything seems to slow down with it. The trade wind abates, the waves lower, and the currents disappear. With every mile traveled, the tailwind becomes slacker and at dawn on the third day, we are completly becalmed. The sea is still with a sleek and oily surface that by day reflects images of the sun and clouds, and by night mirrors the stars. Due to the lack of waves or perhaps due to the complete silence, everything turns somber around us and the ocean seems increasingly larger, like an infinite world to be crossed slyly on tiptoe without drawing attention to ourselves.

At dawn the sky is still serene, then, with the rising sun, the temperature increases and the sky fills with grand, spectacular clouds. In the afternoon, storms of wind and rain start to rage, yet we don't advance. The winds are strong, we have to reef and change a jib sail, both operations that require time and take longer than the winds will permit. We decide instead to lower all the sails and wait in the rain while the storm runs its course, until the blue sky returns, and the winds disappear. We advance very slowly

216

216 bottom The sea lies still
with a surface as sleek as silk,
which by day reflects the sun
and clouds, and by night reflects
the stars.

216-217 Sailors once feared the
equatorial calms more than stormy
seas, their sailing ships remaining
trapped for months, motionless,
and held in a sort of timeless spell.

on an uncertain route that requires us to turn and twist, meanwhile trying to take shelter under a small improvised awning, spending our time reading, looking around, and all the while getting pounded with bucketfuls of sea water. Moving like snails, we cross the equator on the sixth day.

After four days of barely covering more than 20 miles (32 km) in a 24-hour period and just before dawn we hear the sound of small waves against the hull, which wakes us up suddenly. We rush out on deck thinking that perhaps a

ship is passing. Instead, it is the wind making the sea slightly choppy. We hoist the jibs and in the uncertain light of dawn, we start sailing again. We are only moving forward at 3 knots (3.5 m.p.h.) yet after so many days of being almost stationary it seems like we are "exceeding the speed limit." This new wind coming from the south tells tales that come from the other half of the world, the first signs of the southern trade wind that will now never abandon us.

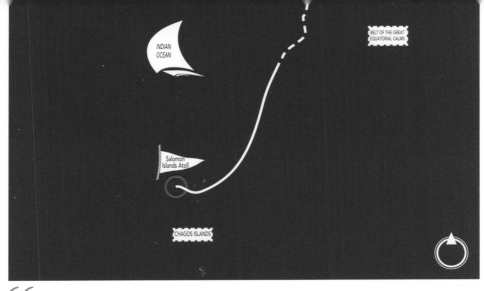

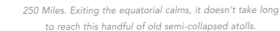

" *250 Miles. Exiting the equatorial calms, it doesn't take long to reach this handful of old semi-collapsed atolls.* "

The Chagos Islands
UNPOLLUTED ATOLLS

On the Salomon Islands atoll, there is a tiny old coral jetty where we land in the dinghy. At the end of the jetty is a Union Jack flag along with a placard welcoming us to BIOT, or British Indian Ocean Territory. Both flag and sign recall those planted on mountaintops in order to indicated newly conquered territory. In the heart of the Indian Ocean, the Chagos Islands, apart from Diego Garcia, are uninhabited and there is no one to control who disembarks on this last piece of the United Kingdom east of the Suez Canal. It wasn't always this way. The islands were inhabited until the beginning of the 1970s when the United States decided to build a strategic naval base here in the Indian Ocean. A place where they could dock submarines, warships, supply ships, aircraft carriers, and all the support services necessary for a rapid intervention task force in the Middle East region. They opted for Diego Garcia, the most isolated atoll in the Chagos, and made an official request to lease it from Great Britain. Twelve hundred people lived on the island, descendants of the lepers and other colonists that had come here

two hundred years before to process copra. For the security of the base, however, the islands had to be uninhabited and without much ceremony the 1,200 inhabitants were deported to Mauritius.

When we arrive here the former inhabitants have been gone for a few decades now and the vegetation has already taken the upper hand over what they had built. Just after disembarking, we find the remains of what were probably the copra storage depots. Further along, a network of little paths still just survives to indicate the way through thick lush green grass to the old residential dwellings. We walk along a slightly wider path than the rest and we come to a wooden house at the edge of a clearing. It is an impressive structure with a raised veranda supported by small, inlaid columns. A gigantic fern now grows through the veranda's skylight. The interior consists of one large room still containing a table, a small shelf with strange wooden objects on it, and a tin cup hanging on a hook. It looks as if the occupants might have been forced to leave very quickly.

There are more houses further down the path. Areas planted with banana trees appear suddenly behind liana vines, semi-covered by flowering bushes and clusters of white orchids. At the end of the road is a church with a memorial plaque with a cross on it and dated 1935. The church façade is tall and narrow like that of a little mountain church and a pothos plant with large green heart-shaped leaves pokes through a rose window over the door. The roof is no longer there and only the walls and the round apse remain, which is slightly raised off the floor. On the sides of the only nave there are three mullioned windows, which still contain glass in blues, yellows, reds, greens, and whites, all leaded. Certainly, these beautiful windows must have been imported from a great distance away and paid for with money from the proceeds of copra production.

218 bottom There are no modern-day transportation links between Chagos and the rest of the world, the only way to get there is on your own boat or on one rented at Gan, the southernmost island in the Maldives.

218-219 During his stopover at the Chagos Archipelago during his circumnavigation on the Beagle, Darwin formulated his theory of atolls as the remains of ancient submerged volcanoes.

219 bottom left Pools of water form within the reef among the coral formations, veritable natural swimming pools, also aquariums where all indigent species are protected.

219 bottom right For a half-century, the Chagos have been uninhabited and the inner atoll lagoons show no signs of pollution or human exploitation.

The Chagos Islands

220 top A ripe coconut may contain more than 16 oz (450 g) of fresh liquid, a treasure in a place where fresh water is in short supply.

220 center On islands without any human presence, the animals inhabiting it don't recognize any potential danger and approach you freely.

220 bottom The coconut crab is a land species that feeds on coconut pulp, successfully cracking open the shell with its deadly and very sharp pincers.

220-221 Always blowing from the east, the trade wind slowly bends the trunks of palm trees growing near the shore so that you can pick coconuts quite easily from some of them.

The Chagos Islands

222 top and 223 bottom left
The islands are now uninhabited
but for 200 years a community of
lepers and other colonists lived
here then left suddenly at the
beginning of the 1970s.

222 bottom The United
Kingdom's flag and a written sign

stand in welcome, reminding
us that we have arrived at a
BIOT, a British Indian Ocean
Territory.

222-223 Nature has taken the
upper hand over what humans
have cultivated and this
plantation of tubers is now

a fine mess through which it
is impossible to move.

223 bottom right This church
has a tall and narrow façade like
that of an alpine church, and a
pothos plant with large green
heart-shaped leaves is growing
through the rose window.

224-225 The first European to see the Seychelles was Vasco de Gama around 1500 and the first to disembark was Alexander Sharpeigh in 1609.

224 bottom An international airport didn't open here in the capital of Mahé until 1971, before that you could only get here by sea.

225 bottom The beach of La Digue island is adorned with rounded, dark granite boulders that form a boundary between the sand and the green vegetation.

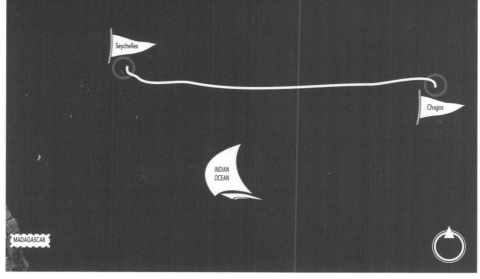

" 1,130 Miles. Nine days with a favorable trade wind and current,
arriving at a mountainous archipelago with small, inaccessible valleys
where the giant coco de mer was concealed from explorers for centuries. "

Seychelles Islands

THE LARGEST SEED IN THE WORLD

The Vallée de Mai (May Valley) in the heart of Praslin Island is the only place in the world where the coco de mer grows, which is a palm tree that holds several world records. It is one of the tallest, has the longest leaves, lives the longest, and produces the largest seed in the world. The excessive dimensions of this coconut, almost 1.75 ft (55 cm) in diameter and weighing just over 66 lb (30 kg), has prevented the species from spreading to other regions. Such a seed certainly cannot be transported by the wind or be ingested by birds to then be deposited in other places as happens with many other plant species. The coco de mer will not float and so can't be carried by waves and currents from one island to another. As a result, this seed germinates only on the ground where it falls.

The first voyagers to reach the Seychelles stopped only on the coasts without penetrating into the valleys and mountains. However, someone happened to find old coco de mer shells on the shore, emptied over time and carried by the seasonal rains and floods downhill. Thinking that this strange fruit had been washed ashore by the sea, they called the unknown tree that produced them *Lodoicea maldivica*, theorizing that they had come from the Maldives. This name was still used even when explorers began to penetrate the island and discovered the Vallée de Mai, which is the small enchanting valley where the *Lodoicea* actually grows.

Discovering the source of this gigantic fruit, news spread and it is easy to imagine the mayhem that ensued. These exceptional coconuts were in high demand all over the world in all sorts of products, often polished, silver-plated, and fashioned into trays and containers. The Seychelles people competed keenly over selling them. However, it could take up to 20 years to obtain fruit from one tree, as they only produce fruit when fully mature. The people anxiously awaited the palm trees' growth so that they could pick coconuts as early and quickly as possible. Ripe coconuts no longer fell and remained on the ground to germinate

as they had for thousands of years and the valley's biological balance was seriously compromised over the course of one century. Fortunately, in 1983, the Vallée de Mai was declared a park and since then no one has been permitted to pick or sell its precious coconuts. Those that ripen on trees are monitored one by one and when one falls it is left on the ground to propagate new palm trees. Only a few dozen coconuts are picked each year by the park rangers and are available only at a very high price and only to those who require them for study or other important work.

We fall within this group, as we need one of these giant coconuts for our documentary. In a park office, we fill out a request form in triplicate then we have to shell out, no pun intended, more than 100 dollars to an employee that signs our receipt and solemnly accompanies us to select our coconut among a dozen that are numbered and lined up against a wall. Along with the coconut, the employee issues us an export permit, a real and proper passport to show customs officers when weighing anchor, and a valid pass to transport our cargo from park storage to the boat. Finally, with the paperwork complete, we may go on our merry way carrying our very large nut.

226 top left The coco de mer palm takes 20 years to mature. Its giant fruit are now carefully monitored and their trade is rigidly controlled by government officials.

Seychelles Islands

226 top right To acquire a coco de mer coconut, you must request authorization and documentation from the park office in order to both transport the coconut from the office and export it to your home country.

226 center The coco de mer coconut does not float and so is not carried by waves and currents from one island to another, consequently this "seed" germinates only on the ground where it falls.

226 bottom Giant sea turtles were once abundant on the islands but were then decimated once people arrived. They are now diligently protected.

226-227 The Vallée de Mai in the heart of Praslin Island is the only spot in the world where the coco de mer palm grows. It is the holder of many records in the botanical world.

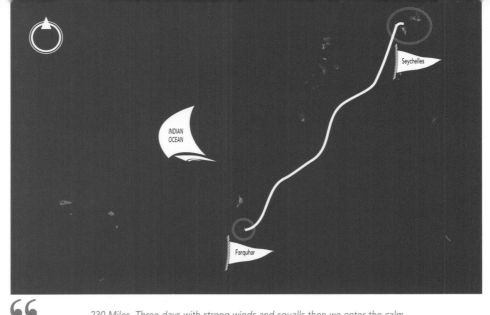

" *230 Miles. Three days with strong winds and squalls then we enter the calm lagoon of Farquhar, an atoll and park where sea turtles, crabs, boobies, gannets, and frigate birds live almost completely undisturbed.* "

Farquhar Atoll
LIVING IN A PARK

Finally after a week of sailing through the rain and against headwinds, the Farquhar atoll appears. The channel passage to enter the lagoon is quite visible within the green coral that, thanks to an unexpected stream of sunlight, stands out in the glossy blue water. We anchor across from a village stretched out over a small green meadow.

Farquhar, along with the Aldabra and Cosmoledo islands, form a marine park belonging to the Seychelles. The capital is hundreds of miles away and very few people live on Farquhar. Leroy, the park ranger, and a dozen other families came here on behalf of the government. Leroy is very proud of his island. He welcomes us and then loads us onto a cart for a tour of the atoll. He explains that since park maintenance costs are so high, the government decided to finance it through the production of copra and they provide a house and travel costs for those who want to come here to work. The work consists of picking 600 coconuts every day, cutting them open, extracting the pulp, and

drying it in the sun to make copra. A fast worker can complete the task in four hours and then be free to go fishing for the rest of the day.

Meanwhile the cart has arrived at the landing strip, which is a belt of land about 16.5 ft (5 m) wide, 33 ft (10 m) long, and full of holes and bumps. We move in closer and discover that the bumps are actually giant sea turtles! "We don't know why, but they love to rest here. Every two weeks when the airplane arrives, we have to run around and clear the airstrip of sea turtles. They weigh almost 450 lb (200 kg) and it takes two teams of four men each to lift and carry them into the brush. But we do it willingly because this is a nature preserve and we have to safeguard the animals from any danger." We continue our tour of the atoll while Leroy points out the plants that once served as timber for building canoes, the irontree and the bread tree, and finally he takes us to the cliffs where frigate birds, boobies, and gannets nest in their thousands. When we return, he invites us to lunch.

We eat beneath the veranda at his home, along with the whole family, around a large table covered with flowers, drinking glasses, and steaming bowls of food. However, the dishes are unrecognizable. He outlines the menu for us: curried sea turtle (protected species) stew, gigantic sea turtle (endangered) in tomato sauce; hearts of palm (a young palm tree is felled just to feed two people) marinated in lime and coconut milk, *birgo latro* or coconut crab (almost extinct) with a strange dark sauce, scrambled frigate bird eggs (he is evidently indifferent that they come here to nest), and hard boiled sea turtle eggs (a similar attitude). Seeing the dumfounded looks on our faces, Leroy seems concerned. "If your religion forbids you to eat something, just eat what your are permitted to eat." What do we do? We eat a large part of what God has blessed us with, besides, the park ranger has already thoughtfully prepared it for us and what's more, it is also very good!

228 bottom Farquhar, along with Aldabra and Cosmoledo Islands, is part of a protected marine preserve and you need a special permit to disembark here.

229 The lagoon at Farquhar is not very deep and coral formations are near the water's surface for the joy of all to see and snap pictures.

Farquhar Atoll

230 and 231 top Normally, boobies and gannets nest on cliffs inaccessible to people and other predators. However, in the Farquhar atoll nests are scattered everywhere.

To maintain the park, the Seychelles government finances it with copra production and provides a house and travel costs to those who want to come here to work.

231 bottom The terns choose the highest part of the beach to lay their eggs and care for their nestlings until the young birds are capable of fishing on their own.

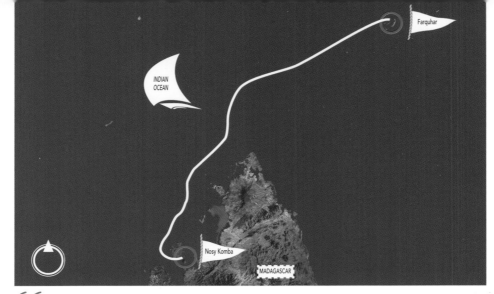

" 450 Miles. Five days, a rapid sail with high waves that disappear once we round the northern tip of Madagascar. "

Nosy Komba

THE SACRED LEMURS

"*Maki, maki, maki….*" Marie emits a melodious call and waves two bananas that she has brought with her in the air. We hear thuds and sounds of branches breaking then a ball of reddish fur darts out of a tree and lands directly on her shoulder. A second later and the lemur is on the ground beside us, completely focused on eating the banana that it has snatched out of the girl's hands. We start shooting video, then another two of them arrive and still more until there are at least a dozen jumping around from one branch to branch, onto the ground, from the ground to our shoulders. They are small lemurs who seem friendly and are definitely lively. The reddish ones, Marie says, are female and the black ones with the white muzzles are males. They all continue to jump around, as we have hidden other bananas under a bush. The frenzy increases as the lemurs jump all around us and as we jump around them trying

to film and photograph them. We take close-ups of their muzzles, detailed shots of their human-like "hands," and follow them in the viewfinder as they jump from one branch to another around the clearing. The lemurs at Nosy Komba are not afraid of people because here they have always been considered sacred, and if some villager wounds one or even just mistreats one, his or her family will become a disgrace to the community. We sailed along the western coast of Madagascar trying to find lemurs to photograph, but other than a few in the tops of trees we weren't successful in finding many really good specimens. These lively characters we encountered just a few miles from the city, free inside this village with its clean, sandy little streets, tidy huts, and clearings where red coffee beans and darker cocoa beans are laid out in the sun to dry. The empty clearing just outside the village is great, but we must enter further into the forest to photograph the lemurs in their true environment. Although Marie tries to hold us back we delve deeper into the brush just outside the clearing. There is no path and we are not dressed properly, but we only need to move just a few yards further into the forest to get some good shots. We go a bit further into the bushes and start to feel a nagging itch on our skin that quickly changes to stinging. Maybe there are red ants here but we don't see any. But the itching sensation becomes more intense, like a hundred stinging nettles. We begin to feel like we're on fire. We emerge, running out of the bush to find Marie laughing, pointing at a bush with unfamiliar grayish pods on it. The area around us is full of bushes just like this one. "Legend says that these bushes are the guardians of the lemurs, they can come into the village undisturbed, but anyone who follows the lemurs back into the forest will be stabbed by the thorns on these pods."

232 bottom In these small outrigger canoes equipped with sail and lift net, the fishermen cruise along the coast without ever venturing out to challenge the currents in the Mozambique Channel.

233 The word lemurs comes from the Latin lemures, *meaning "spirits of the night" and many species, in fact, have nocturnal habits and large eyes that reflect light.*

Nosy Komba

234 top All you need is an old can, some pieces of wood, a few bottle caps, and a stick to build a toy when you can't buy one.

234 center Because of the difficulty in navigating the Mozambique Channel, the Malagasy population is not of African origin, rather they have Asiatic and even Polynesian roots.

234 bottom To avoid getting their faces burned by the equatorial sun, young women apply a clay mask mixed with coconut milk.

234-235 Lemurs in Nosy Komba are not afraid of people because they have always been considered sacred here and are revered, protected, and coddled.

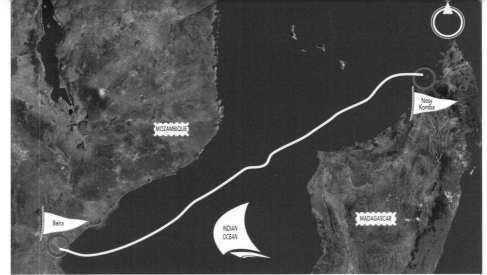

"1,250 Miles. Twelve days to journey through the Mozambique Channel with the current off Mozambique complicating navigation. To escape a cyclone, we enter a large bay then a river near the old city of Beira."

Beira

AN EXPOSED COASTLINE

Beira is on a river estuary behind a large bay on the coast of Mozambique. On the city-side shore there is a kind of dock. In any other situation we would have avoided it as chaotic ports of this kind aren't good places for a sailboat such as ours. In particular, tugs tow enormous barges with no concern for buffets and collisions, both given and received. Just one false or careless move and a sailboat could end up crushed. We don't have the dinghy now and that would be the only way to disembark. So we enter the docking area and moor the boat by tying it off to the side of a tugboat with the ONU flag, which is in turn tied to the side of a larger ship, which is coupled to yet another. We are in the fourth row of boats, far from land with a potentially disastrous chain of ships between the wharf and us. In order to get there, we have to climb over all of the ships, the last one with a ship rail about ten feet above the wharf. We have to put on long pants and clean T-shirts to present ourselves to the customs officials, but even

before setting foot on land our clothes look like those worn by longshoremen.

Passports, stamps, forms to fill out in triplicate and in just two hours all is completed. We have obtained authorization to tour the city. We exchange money, find the market, stock up on supplies, and purchase water and diesel fuel. We are able to find everything but the city is frantically busy and we must obtain a special permit for both the diesel and water. Thus, we spend our time completing our errands and when we return to the port, the afternoon has already wasted away. Loaded down with bags and sacks, we climb up over the side of the first ship and are paralyzed by shock. The sea has disappeared. The port is dry, completely drained as if a gigantic pump had suctioned off all of the water. Hundreds of boats, barges, ships, and small fishing boats lie "aground," stretched out in the mud.

We drop our shopping bags and run, climbing over ships' rails, running up steps, passing from one deck to the next towards the ONU tug behind which our boat is hiding. We are already imagining the worst, the lines torn apart, the boat balancing on its keel, maybe even fallen over on its side. Instead, we just find it sitting a bit cockeyed, semi-submerged in the mud with the masts leaning to one side but still intact. If we thought to check the tide charts before stopping over here, we would have discovered that the tidal range along the coast of Mozambique exceeds 13 ft (4 m). At low tide, the water recedes, leaving all docked boats lying in a semi-liquid soft "magma" that looks like chocolate pudding. We can do nothing except double our mooring lines and wait for the water that should return after just two hours. It starts to return first as a yellowish rivulet, then a small brown stream, and finally a river that refills the port as, one by one, ships again start rocking at their moorings as if nothing happened at all.

236 bottom The women's colored sarongs are vividly colored, as are the boats, reflecting the sunny nature of the inhabitants of Mozambique.

236-237 Wooden canoes cruise through a dark sea clouded with sediment carried from the river that, according to the season, goes north or south.

237 bottom right Rivers coming from Africa's interior to the Indian Ocean pour enormous quantities of sand into the sea, modifying the coastline over time.

237 bottom left The market on the river's shore is one of the centers of daily activity here at Beira.

Fishermen come here with their fresh catch as well as women with fruits and vegetables to sell.

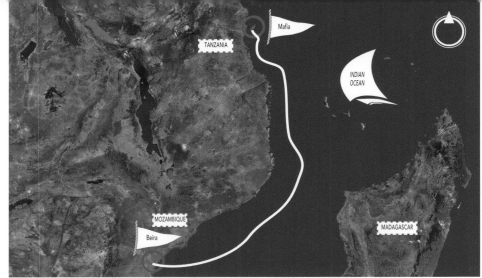

> *1,300 Miles. Two weeks northward to arrive at a coral island where everyone's life is influenced by the tides and by the old wooden dhow ships.*

Mafia Island

THE LAST SAILBOAT CROSSING

Chole Island is a green oasis planted in the sea half a mile southeast of Mafia Island. The inhabitants of its only village make a living by cultivating papayas, maize, pineapples, tapioca, and mangoes, which they take to sell at the market on Mafia Island. There is no school on Chole and the children must go to Mafia, as must anyone who needs to see a doctor or go to the hospital. For all these comings and goings, the only means of transport between the smaller and larger island is a ferry. Over the years and throughout many seas, we have encountered all kinds of ferryboat and all types of passengers, from the ferries running between Singapore and Indonesia to

tramp steamers chugging, if not struggling, from one island to the next in the scattered Pacific archipelagos. However, a ferryboat such as this we have never seen before. It is an old *dhow* that has definitely seen better days. It sets sail at the crack of dawn with the wind and current its only means of propulsion, and goes back and forth all day between Chole and Mafia. The *dhow* transports its human cargo in a wooden hull dried out by the sun and battered by the years, a cotton sail that displays clearly its many repairs, a gray and gnarled mast, a heavy external rudder, and a long pole for dealing with any potentially difficult situations. Embarkation and disembarkation locations change according to the time of day. At low tide, the ferry is compelled to stop more than 325 ft (100 m) from the shore. When this happens a procession of people winds out from the shore, carrying multi-colored bundles, baggage of every kind, including animals, and moves slowly through the progressively deeper water until they reach the boat. Once everyone is on board, the old *dhow* raises its sail and slogs towards the opposite shore to unload its passengers, baggage, and animals, then it takes on another full load for the return voyage. The first passengers in the morning are children. They go to school dressed in uniforms with short blue pants or skirts, white shirts, and bare feet. Later, it is the women's turn. They are wrapped in vibrant-colored sarongs of red, yellow, green, and black, with baskets and bundles of fruit to sell at the market. Then throughout the day there are the comings and goings of people with all kinds of baggage and cargo, such as chickens, goats, and even bicycles, until late afternoon when the children return at sunset. The old dhow then finally drops its primitive anchor and rests, waiting for the next day to arrive. The price of passage is just a few cents and the length of the voyage is unpredictable, depending on the wind and, above all, on the currents linked with the tide. Occasionally, it even takes an hour to travel the short distance between Chole and Mafia, which is longer than it takes the small propjet to fly from Mafia to Dar es Salaam.

238 center To return home after selling fruit, women wait on the beach at Mafia Island for the ferry to pick them up.

238 bottom A traditional boat of the Arabian Peninsula and eastern Africa, the dhow has been used for centuries for fishing and other trades.

238-239 With the southwestern monsoon, meteorological conditions along the coast of Africa are remarkable, including dry air, sun, and wind, with no precipitation at all.

239 bottom Coconut palms may grow in a poor, thin soil layer, like that found on the sandy, narrow strip of land of an atoll.

Mafia Island

240 top and 240-241 To fish from a dhow, you must wait for high tide, otherwise there is not enough water to float the boat.

240 top center This coral remains uncovered as the tide retreats, however, exposure to air for several minutes a day doesn't seem to cause it harm.

240 bottom center The Linckia laevigata is the very common blue starfish that lives in the coral reef in just a few inches of water.

240 bottom and 241 bottom With a wooden hull dried out by the sun and battered by the years, as well as a cotton sail displaying its many repairs, the dhow ferry transports its precious human cargo to wherever they need to go.

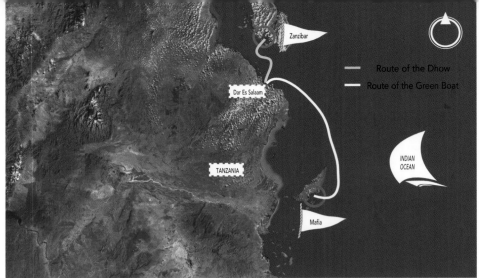

110 Miles. Two days. The scent of cloves carried by the monsoon wafts up to 10 miles (16 km) off the coast.

Zanzibar

THE PORT OF *DHOWS*

Hulls grayed by the sun and coarse-textured cotton sails now yellowed. Sweat and dust covers an incredible group of black, semi-naked longshoremen who form a colorful and disturbing throng that would probably have looked the same centuries ago. This is the old port of Dar es Salaam where sailing *dhows* depart for their commute to Zanzibar.

The *dhows* are massive boats up to 66 ft (20 m) long, just like those that reached the coast of Africa a thousand years ago, gaining access to Mediterranean ports, carrying valuable cargo destined for people in the north and the sultans in the Orient. Today, they carry sacks of maize, zebu, cylinders of gas, and often even cars. "If you want to embark, you have to hide," the boss of one of the *dhows* tells us, "because boarding foreigners is prohibited." So we start our adventure hidden inside a tiny wooden launch on the deck of the *dhow*, spending the afternoon as invisible people spying on the loading and unloading of dozens of ships' holds as they arrive from and leave for who knows where, waiting for night to fall. A line of longshoremen is finishing up loading cargo onto our ship. Each man has about a 110-lb (50 kg) sack of maize on his shoulders. What surrounds us is a world of desperate people. Our safety is completely entrusted to the goodwill of those who, without even knowing us, have agreed to transport us hidden as stowaways. If something were to happen, no one would know, and we would disappear into oblivion. At dawn the crowd disperses and we can come

out into the open to observe departure operations.

The sail rises upward in jerks, hoisted onto the spar with the joint efforts of all the men on board, chanting to maintain a rhythm in their task. The immense sail opens against the dark sky and the boat begins to move silently over the still waters of the port, grazing nearby boats as it heads towards the exit and the channel leading to the ocean. Outside the port, the sea envelops us and we are cloaked in the night while the wind increases and the ship's pace quickens. The sea is full of shallows but these men, who have never even seen a nautical map, accurately guesstimate the correct route through, finding their way based on seemingly mysterious signs of which only they are aware. Once off the coast with no danger in sight, the crew gathers and we all dine together by the light of an oil lamp. We eat a white polenta of sorts, flavored with a very spicy red sauce. We fall asleep on sacks of maize and it seems as if only a few minutes have passed before we wake up to the sound of the sail being lowered by hand.

The scent of cloves reveals where the old port is hidden, packed with large wooden sailing ships. We slip away, hugging the old walls of the city. The large buildings, lace-like patterned bastions, mosques, and Arabic-style façades are testimony to the port's past grandeur and splendor. This is the same architectural opulence that awaited boats full of slaves just 200 years ago. It is the same magnificence that gave rise to the maxim that when you play the flute in Zanzibar, all of Africa dances.

242-243 *Depending on the monsoon, gusts of wind come from the southwest or northeast. Zanzibar's coast is always downwind, sheltered from oceanic waves.*

243 bottom left *A scent of cloves wafts through the air from the inlet where the old port hides, packed with large sailing ships and small launches.*

243 bottom right *These massive boats are the same as those that went up the coast of Africa a thousand years ago to reach Mediterranean ports with their valuable goods.*

243

244-245, 245 top and 245 bottom Buildings with latticework, ramparts, and mosques are testimonies to the past grandeur when it was said that when someone played the flute in Zanzibar, all of Africa danced.

245 center Dhows have always sailed along the African coast and through the Red Sea, arriving at the Arabian Peninsula and navigating north or south depending on the monsoon.

Zanzibar

246-247 and 247 top Boats stop at the edge of the coral reef at any time during the day, but you must walk through the seawater to reach them.

246 bottom Fishermen lay out their nets that will float out to the edge of the coral reef once the tide flows back to the sea.

Zanzibar

247 center Zanzibar overlooks
and lives from the sea, with
seaweed and fish drying in the
sun, the former to be exported
and the latter to be preserved for
leaner times.

247 bottom Marine borers,
worms that feed on the wood
of the hull, can be combated
with careful doses of fire so as
to not compromise the boat's
keel.

248-249 and 248 bottom left After a while the birds got used to us and would land and approach fearlessly, so that we could film and photograph them repeatedly.

248 bottom right The Sula dactylatra, known as the masked booby, has a black strip around its eyes that looks like a Venetian carnival mask.

249 bottom Millions of birds obscure the sun as they rise in flight, cawing, milling around our heads, and bombarding us with all they've got.

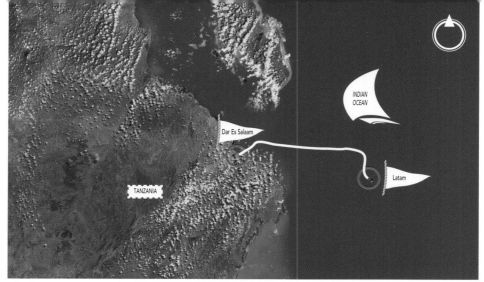
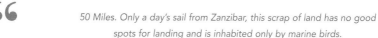

" *50 Miles. Only a day's sail from Zanzibar, this scrap of land has no good spots for landing and is inhabited only by marine birds.* "

Latam

THE ISLAND OF BIRDS

The island of Latam is not much more than a huge boulder in the midst of the ocean, 80 miles (130 km) from Zanzibar. Looking at it on the map, all alone in the ocean, it seems just a promising solitary anchorage in the clear, clean water of the open sea. But when we see it appear in the clear morning light, we understand that it has much more to offer. From a distance we can already see that the sky over Latam is thick with little black dots that come together and separate, forming strange black splotches that condense and dissolve like plumes of smoke. They are, in fact, enormous flocks of birds, all seeming to originate from this tiny land.

We approach until we reach an area quite close to these swirling flocks. The island is too small to provide effective protection from the waves, but we drop anchor anyway, just over 218 yards (200 m) from the shore. The boat is rocking, rolling, and riding large waves as if we were still sailing. We put the dinghy in the sea among the waves and with some gymnastic moves we load it with the oars and kedge anchor, transferring our bags with video cameras and tripod aboard. We approach the island on the almost 7-ft (2-m) high breakers that envelop the island in an imposing ribbon of foam. We haven't yet attempted a landing in these conditions and try to remember how the Polynesians disembarked in similar conditions: waiting for the right wave sequence, counting the waves, two, three…five…seven…and so on and so forth, then launching themselves forward after the largest wave. We also launch ourselves forward after a wave of majestic proportions. With lightweight and streamlined canoes, the Polynesians let themselves be carried by the waves, balancing on the crests until they landed on the sand beyond any tidal backwash. We rear up in our awkward and heavy dinghy as the stern rises, maneuvering the prow into the hollow between the waves, then we cross and keep one inflatable side of the dinghy low and the

other high, while the foaming mass of water pushes us from behind. Seconds later and the sand is scratching our skin and the heavy weight of our dinghy is bearing down on our heads. However, what really counts is what is waiting for us on dry land.

The whole island is literally covered with birds, eggs, chicks, female birds sitting on their eggs, and adult birds regurgitating fish to feed their young. We walk around dazed and bewildered, wandering aimlessly in 90-degree heat, intruders in a world of birds. Millions of birds rise upward in flight, cawing, spinning around our heads, and dive-bombing us with all they have. Millions of others remain on the ground because they don't yet know how to fly, squawking and watching us anxiously. From an egg suddenly abandoned on the sand, a very weak chick breaks out chirping, two faint cracks in its shell indicating the point where its beak began to peck away towards new life. After just a half hour, the animals get used to us, landing and approaching fearlessly. We shoot lots of video and stills, while at just over 218 ft (65 m) away from us our boat awaits us, pitching and swaying frighteningly at its mooring.

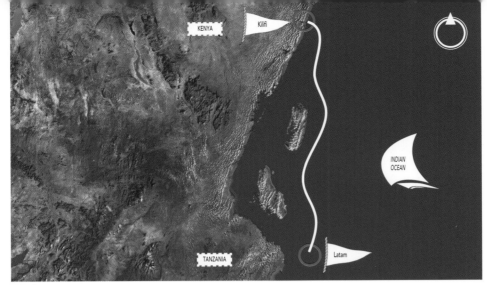

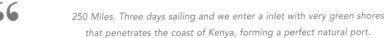

> *250 Miles. Three days sailing and we enter a inlet with very green shores that penetrates the coast of Kenya, forming a perfect natural port.*

Kilifi

THE BRIDGE OVER THE INLET

We finally have the entrance to the inlet in sight. Moving past the last bank of coral, we can head towards the entrance, towards the heart of this strip of sea that cuts through the land for several miles. We navigate between two outcrops covered in almond trees, casuarinas evergreen shrubs, and trees with a floral scent that wafts through the air as far as our boat. Twenty years ago this inlet still interrupted the coastline road that ran from Tanzania, through Kenya, and reached beyond the border of Somalia. Here at Kilifi you had to stop and wait for the ferry to reach the opposite shore and continue the trip. The road climbed uphill and only reached sea level in an abrupt curving descent, with the water seeming to appear suddenly. The ribbon of road ended at the sea as if its path should continue by force beneath the seafloor to then reemerge on the opposite side. Along the descent you had to wait until the ferry would arrive and allow its cargo of people, crates, bundles,

goats, trucks bound together with iron cabling, minibuses, and beat-up cars to discharge and disembark along the dirt road. You had to wait at least for an hour and during this time you took the opportunity to observe everything around you. There were huts made of mud with lit fires inside, children grazing their goats, girls wrapped in colorful sarongs, women with newborns slung in fabric strapped to their backs, and old people selling cashews in paper cones. A hectic and authentic piece of Africa accessible to whoever paused to take it all in. A bridge has now been built between the two banks of the inlet. It appears suddenly in front of us blocking our path, enormous and out of place like a hard grey plastic Lego piece inserted into a soft velvety plasticine landscape.

Our nautical chart doesn't alert us to its existence, doesn't say how high it is, and doesn't indicate how to pass beneath it. We try to sail under it at low tide when the water level has dropped and the current stops completely, so that in case of any problems we could reverse direction and move on another way. When that moment arrives, with one of us at the rudder and the other at the mast, we go ahead and try. At the beginning, we are very near the left shore and have to avoid a bank of coral, passing under a line of electrical cabling where they are at the higher point above the water. We get to the middle of the waterway and head towards the center of the bridge where its span is higher. The top of our 60-ft mast (18-m) sways with the movement of the boat and, from the deck we can't tell if we are too tall to pass beneath. We advance very slowly, yard by yard, uncertainly and even doubtfully. Up on the bridge, the colorful pedestrian traffic has stopped and everyone leans over to observe the big event of the day. "You've got it, my friend, *hakuna matata*," someone shouts. We find ourselves in the humid and somewhat cold shadows of the bridge's span, under the roadway that shakes and rumbles with the passage of vehicles. The sun then returns to warm up our skin and we are finally free as the boat is inundated with light, and we may head towards a spot to anchor.

250 bottom The Pillar of Vasco de Gama was erected in 1498 where Malindi now rises up, in one of the few places where the Portuguese man's expedition was welcomed.

250-251 The Kilifi bridge replaced the old ferry crossing that until the end of the 1980s transferred goods and passengers from one shore to the other.

251 bottom The inlet at Kilifi is a strip of seawater that wounds the land, interrupting the smooth sweep of the coastline, running from the border with Tanzania all the way to Somalia.

252-253 Danger during a voyage doesn't always come from the sea, for example, passing under a bridge, it may also come from above.

251

254-255 Rocky and whipped by the wind, this arid island doesn't produce anything, but the sea around it provides the islanders with an inexhaustible and valuable resource.

254 bottom Socotra was a pirate cove for centuries, then a Soviet naval base was built here and only a few years ago stopovers were prohibited.

255 bottom Adenium socotranum or desert rose is a very strange tree endemic to the island that has a structure capable of resisting the high winds of this region.

> 1,300 Miles. After 12 days of sailing some distance from the coast of Somalia for security reasons, we give in to the temptation of stopping at Socotra despite the dubious reputation of the island.

Socotra

WINDY ISLAND

A car appears on the dusty road. It is sort of a pale yellow, Jeep-type vehicle, kicking up clumps of dirt as it heads straight for us. It stops and two men dressed in light-colored, long loose robes and wearing embroidered skullcaps get out. With friendly but insistent gestures, they ask us to follow them. "Mudir," says one of them. We have to go see their leader! We can do nothing other than consent, starting to regret stopping here at Socotra, an island that has always been a base for pirates and where, until just a few years ago, it was prohibited to land.

We find ourselves holding on tight inside their vehicle, thrown around as we ride over enormous potholes, passing houses made of stone, disorderly goats fleeing, and children looking at us as if we have come from Mars as we travel through the narrow streets of Hadiboo, the only village on the island. After a few sharp bends and more jostling, the Jeep stops in front of a large white building with four turrets on top. We are led through a small door and find ourselves in a white and spacious room. There are many people sitting on mats against the walls, all seeming to be waiting expectantly. In the back of the room a mountain of cushions accommodates what seems undeniably to be their leader. He is tall and imposing and although seated his head towers over everyone else. He wears a brightly colored dhoti and a blousy shirt of white cotton. Perhaps to hold up his dhoti, he has a leather belt beneath the shirt, inside which he's slipped a big black pistol, which rests directly over his rib cage. Our fear increases. The person accompanying us makes a deep bow to the floor and then disappears, slithering like a snake through the small door where we entered. We are alone in the center of the room and everyone is watching us.

Two cushions and a tray with two glasses of steaming tea are provided. "I saw you arrive," the chief begins, offering us

a reassuring smile and surprising us with clear and fluent English. He wants to know where we are from and why we have landed at Socotra. We answer that we have come here because we thought that it was an interesting island, although we haven't come here to see anyone in particular. He wants to know if we are familiar with Yemen, what other countries we have visited and, given that the list is long, he wants our opinion about Socotra. We say that we'd just arrived the day before and haven't yet seen much, but maintain that it looks very beautiful and take a chance by saying that we would like to see more of it. "You may stay here as long as you like and see everything you wish to see. If you need something, let me know personally. Do you need any food, water, or fuel?" He gives us another smile and claps his hands. A woman appears with a straw basket containing a papaya, a huge pineapple, and two bunches of bananas. "These come from the garden here and are some of the few things that the island produces."

256-257 and 257 *From May to October during the months of the southwestern monsoon, the wind coming from the hottest regions of Africa's interior may* reach up to 60 knots (70 m.p.h./ 112 km/h), carrying with it sand that modifies the landscape and transforms the beaches into dunes.

Socotra

258-259 Seagulls covering the beaches and cliffs on Socotra during the winter season come here to flee the cold of Siberia.

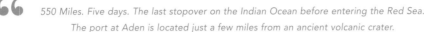

> 550 Miles. Five days. The last stopover on the Indian Ocean before entering the Red Sea.
> The port at Aden is located just a few miles from an ancient volcanic crater.

Aden

GATEWAY TO THE RED SEA

The engine doesn't seem to know how to start. It makes a strange sound, a gurgling, as if it were flooded with water. A good amount of water gushes out of it when we unscrew the injectors to inspect it. We won't attempt to repair it in the middle of the ocean, but when we reach Aden, and so we go ahead and sail into the port. However, it is not ideal to sail into a busy commercial port. Enormous ships towed by powerful tugboats take precedence over everyone else. Adding to all this is a multitude of smaller boats, including rusty fishing steamers, old wooden freighters, and smaller boats that wander from one shore to another following chaotic routes and somewhat suspicious comings and goings. The wind is light but unfavorable.

The sweeping channel, marked by red and green buoys, is less than 700 ft (215 m) wide and we have to enter the waterway on the wind to get inside the port. We advance slowly with sails that graze the sides of gigantic ships, while our masts don't even reach the height of their lowest decks. A launch cuts us off and, avoiding it, we lose a large part of the distance already traveled. Then an ugly boat full of fishermen shouting and gesticulating passes, making us understand that their net has already been cast into the water. We also try to explain that our motor isn't working. It takes us a couple of hours to reach a small basin where we drop anchor and relax. We can finally look at what is around us. On land, the dominant color is that of the desert, and there are dusty streets and houses, with the old volcano in the distance. We disembark into the burning heat of the afternoon. We don't see a living soul apart from several old rickety automobiles that pass us, raising clouds of dust. In this desert city, we are desperate to find someone to repair the boat's engine. Ali is the enterprising taxi driver that welcomes us from the oven-baked street. He doesn't seem to want to understand that we need him to take us to customs officials and to find a mechanic. "We'll think about that tomorrow. Those are things that you should do in the morning. Now, we're going to see Crater." At the old city, Crater, we tour the streets of the market among dusty shops that sell coal and corn seed. We end up in some kind of restaurant where a sweaty cook prepares small bundles of pasta stuffed with an egg hidden inside – a luxury after a 20-day crossing. The next day, we even meet a mechanic and discover that Ali was right. In Aden, things are only taken care of in the morning because everything closes down completely in the afternoon. The people of Yemen make use of the *khat* or *Catha edulis.* This is a small shrub with very green and tender leaves that people keep in their mouths for hours, rolled up into a ball. A large stall in Crater's market is dedicated to selling *khat.* Evidently all of the men and almost all of the women have cheeks bulging from a ball of leaves in their mouths. The effect of *khat* on Aden's inhabitants is to induce an apathetic state of happiness, even with the heat beating down from the early hours of the afternoon.

260 bottom One section of the market at Crater is dedicated to the sale of khat, Catha edulis, a plant with tender leaves that people chew and keep in their mouths for hours.

260-261 On land, the dominant color is the gray of the desert and, among the dusty streets with the old volcano in the distance, the white houses stand out starkly.

261 bottom There are chaotic and often suspicious comings and goings at the port of Aden, with enormous ships flanked by a multitude of smaller patched and rusty boats.

262-263 *Sailing the Red Sea is one of the most demanding voyages throughout our world tour, with its strong headwinds, and short and choppy waves.*

262 bottom left *The Hanish Islands are covered by black earth with no water or vegetation, and are aligned along the Red Sea axis.*

262 bottom right *A small group of seagulls observe the scene from the nearby rocks, waiting to hurl themselves onto any shark remains left unattended.*

263 bottom *Fishermen come from Yemen with boats loaded with barrels of water and fuel, some sacks of rice, flour, some sugar, tea, and tobacco.*

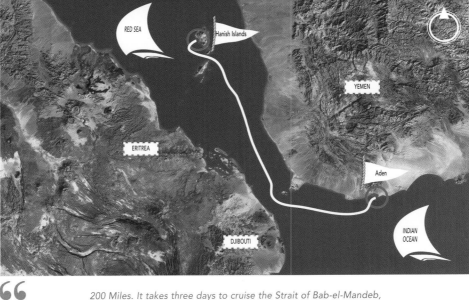
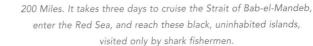

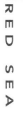

200 Miles. It takes three days to cruise the Strait of Bab-el-Mandeb, enter the Red Sea, and reach these black, uninhabited islands, visited only by shark fishermen.

Hanish Islands

SHARK FISHERMEN

Halfway between Bab-el-Mandeb and Eritrea are the Hanish Islands. The land is black and inhospitable with no water and no vegetation. We anchor at South West Bay just off a small beach where we see a hut made from leafy branches. As we are landing, a green and blue painted boat full of fishermen appears from behind the island heading towards the same beach. When we arrive, the men have already unloaded their catch of the day, made up of sharks and sharks only! The oldest fisherman comes to greet us while the others begin to clean their prey. They cut off the fins and tails then the head and finally carve out two gigantic filets from the carcasses, putting them all out to dry on the black rocks away from the sandy beach. A small group of boobies and gannets survey the scene, cawing and flying in concentric circles, waiting for their opportunity to attack any bits and pieces left unattended.

When the shark meat has been dealt with, Fethini, the oldest, motions us over to the shade of their hut. The others remain in the water washing themselves off then change the tattered clothing they're wearing and we then see them throw themselves prostrate on the ground in a small open space bordered by white shells, oriented to the northeast. It is their makeshift mosque. At the end of the day, they thank Allah for giving them life, for continued life, and certainly for the good catch. A good catch for these men is the shark fins and tails. It is for this reason that throughout the Red Sea and in a large part of the Indian Ocean, sharks are caught indiscriminately. Their fins, worth 24 dollars per kilo (almost 2.25 lb), pass through an intermediary chain, reaching Singapore where they are processed, then finally they arrive on Chinese and Japanese tables. On other islands, we have seen miles of beach entirely covered with shark carcasses, with only their fins and tails removed, and left to rot in the sun.

While the fishermen prepare tea, Fethini tells us about their work. He and the boys come from Moka, 55 miles (88 km) east along the coast of Yemen. They come in a boat loaded with barrels of water and gasoline, some sacks of rice, flour, some sugar, tea, and tobacco. They go out to sea every day, pull in nets cast out the day before, harvest any sharks, repair their nets, and cast them back out into the water. They then return to their ugly little hut made of leafy branches, clean the fish, pray, eat, and go to sleep. At dawn the next day, it starts all over again and this continues for a couple of months until they use up their water and fuel. They then load the empty barrels onto their boat, along with the bags of shark fins/tails and dried meat, and return to Moka. They stay long enough to sell their catch to Arab and Chinese merchants, greet their families, and buy more supplies, then it is time to depart for the Hanish Islands once again. It is a tough existence that only becomes harder as the population of sharks steadily declines due to this absurd, short-sighted, and indiscriminate hunting of these majestic marine animals.

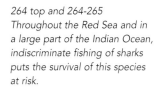

Hanish Islands

264 top and 264-265
Throughout the Red Sea and in
a large part of the Indian Ocean,
indiscriminate fishing of sharks
puts the survival of this species
at risk.

264 center The fishermen cut off
the fins and tail, then the head
and finally the carcass remains,
but they don't even waste the
entrails as they serve as a good
antifouling agent for the boats.

264 bottom Gigantic filets
carved from the sharks are
sprinkled with rock salt and put
out to dry on the black rocks
away from the sandy beach.

265 bottom Through a chain of
intermediaries, dried fins will be
delivered as far away as
Singapore and from there, will
take another journey to satisfy
a high demand in China and
Japan.

264

266-267 Disembarking, we don't see anyone, just a colony of millions of birds that live undisturbed on this flat and rocky terrain.

266 bottom left In this colorless landscape and under this very colorful structure, a chief of one of the island tribes rests.

266 bottom right and 267 bottom Tenacious Eritrean fishermen move continuously from the islands to the coast in

their old wooden sambuks, the traditional boats that have always shuttled from the African coast to Arabia, now Saudi Arabia.

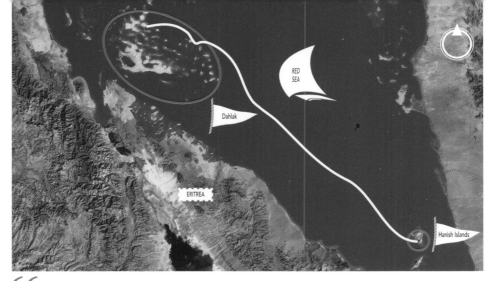

" *180 Miles. Two days sailing and we arrive at an archipelago of 120 islands where slave merchants once stopped over with their precious cargo.* "

Dahlak

A WORLD TO DISCOVER

According to our 1938 Touring Club of Italy guide, there should be some subterranean cisterns at Dahlak Kebir, which were excavated when the island was a base for the slave trade between Africa and Saudi Arabia. When we disembark we don't see a soul, just colonies of many thousands of birds. We push onward over a flat and rocky terrain at the end of which a small village appears at the base of an arid hillock. A group of women wrapped in discolored, faded, gauzy fabric, revealing their long dark-skinned arms, welcomes us. They smile, gesticulate, and attempt to communicate with us in an unknown dialect, interspersed with a few words of Arabic as they nudge us along, escorting us to their mud houses built on the black earth. They invite us to sit underneath a wooden baldachin on two cushions while men dressed in white and semi-nude children come forward. These people belong to the Afar tribe and they proudly show us the carefully made carvings on the corners of the baldachin. These people are semi-nomadic and have always moved freely between Sudan and Eritrea, along the coast and among the islands, without being recognized as citizens of either country. They offer us their coffee, which is black, very sweet, and full of ginger.

Around us stretches away a yellow-colored, arid plain with few undulations and just enough bushes for camels to browse. We try to ask our hosts where the cisterns are, miming digging holes in the ground, and using the Arabic word *maa*, which means water. They lead us down a path along which there are groups of girls with water vessels balanced on their heads. We reach a small valley near to the sea with a series of holes in the ground in the shade of a line of palm trees. They aren't the cisterns we are looking for, but it is a magnificent spot. A soft and delicate carpet of green grass confirms the presence of water. Many of the holes are dry but some

do have small pools of muddy, brown water at the bottom, containing fish and tadpoles. In this place where it never rains, the water is soft and sweet, and tastes better than we expected.

A week later in Sarad, further to the south, we find the ancient cisterns. They are caves covered by a stone vault, excavated more than 1,000 years ago to provide water for the slaves who were brought through here from Africa on their way to the markets in Saudi Arabia, Egypt, Yemen, and India. The water still looks transparent at the bottom of the cisterns. In the same neighborhood there is also a necropolis with a stone perimeter wall and hundreds of well-preserved tombs, including several carved and sculpted tombstones. Still partially intact arches and columns, carved with Arabic, Persian, and Farsi inscriptions, are silhouetted against the sky throughout the necropolis. An old man appearing from nowhere makes us understand that he is the guardian here. He tells us all sorts of things and we think he wants money. Instead, he only wants to warn us that stones may not be removed from here as they belong to the people of Eritrea!

268-269 The inhabitants of the Dahlak Archipelago live in villages of stone structures with a few goats and camels, speak Tigrinya and Arabic, and even some Italian as well.

269 Subterranean caves covered by a stone vault, still partially intact arches, and several carved or sculpted tombstones with Arabic or Persian inscriptions are up to a thousand years old.

Dahlak

270-271 and 271 At the end of the 19th century the Dahlak Archipelago became an Italian Colonial Protectorate and now, after Eritrea's independence, it is a natural preserve.

During the very long civil war between Eritrea and Ethiopia, the Dahlak islands were declared off-limits and were only saved by tourism, which at times was not very sustainable.

Dahlak

272-273 Although many people speak Italian on Massawa and the restaurants offer Italian food, the prevailing architecture and urban infrastructure are Arabic in style.

272 bottom left Massawa rises up over a lagoon with two primary islands, Massawa and Taulud, one of which accommodates the Haile Selassie Palace.

272 bottom right and 273 bottom Partially collapsed walls riddled with bullet holes still show the signs left by Ethiopian machineguns during the civil war.

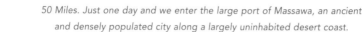

"50 Miles. Just one day and we enter the large port of Massawa, an ancient and densely populated city along a largely uninhabited desert coast."

Massawa

THE SHEEP TRADE

Old black and white photos are hanging on the wall in a bar, including a passenger ship with bunting moored alongside a wharf with plants and flowers, a beachfront promenade with luxury cars, bars with small tables and umbrellas outside, men dressed in white with straw hats, and officials in uniform. The photos date back to the 1950s. There are other photos on the opposite wall of shipwrecks in the port, the customs offices with walls riddled with bullet holes, the white, partly collapsing façade of the Central Bank, and the starry-sky dome ceiling of the Haile Selassie Palace ripped open by cannon fire. These photos date from the 1990s. Massawa has been rebuilt over the last decade. The port has been cleared of ship wreckage, the debris cleaned up off the streets, the buildings patched and whitened with lime, the railroad to Asmara put back into operation, but the splendor of the 1950s has not returned. Eritrea has other priorities for now.

However, everything is going well at Massawa. The people are kind and considerate, though proud and tough as well. Many of them speak Italian and the bars and restaurants remind us of those of our childhood with strips of multi-colored plastic hanging over the doorways, small pastel-colored formica tables, and round-shaped coffee machines. Even the Italian food reminds us of years past with baked pasta, roasted chicken, stuffed peppers, and even an egg sandwich! The architecture and the urban infrastructure of this lagoon city are Arabic in nature, however. In the heart of Massawa, the dense and narrow streets intertwine in a *kasbah* and the ground floors of residential dwellings alternate with shops selling just about everything. On summer nights, beds are brought outside and it looks like you're walking into a story set of the Italian comics series *Corto Maltese*.

The traditional elder wood *sambuk* boats cross from one part of the port to the other, transporting goods and people. There are boats of all sizes here, the largest travel towards Dalak and Saudi Arabia, as this place has always been a bridge between Africa and Asia. On some mornings, the pier is invaded by flocks of bleating sheep, fearfully expectant, as they wait to be crowded on board *sambuks* lined up along the docks. According to the Koran, every believer must sacrifice a sheep by killing it with his or her own hands during the pilgrimage to Mecca.

There aren't any sheep in Saudi Arabia and so a thriving trade has sprung up between the shores of the Red Sea. Each *sambuk* transports hundreds of sheep and we can read the terror in those hundreds of eyes, packed onto the unstable deck of the boat, as we watch this sight we've never encountered before. The same kind of terror also once filled the eyes of slaves departing from this same port in the same kind of boats.

274-275, 275 center and bottom
The Koran says that every believer
making the pilgrimage to Mecca
must sacrifice a sheep, giving rise to
a flourishing sheep trade between
the two shores of the Red Sea.

275 top In the heart of Massawa,
the dense and narrow streets
intertwine as in a kasbah and on
the ground floor, residential
dwellings alternate with shops
selling just about everything.

Massawa

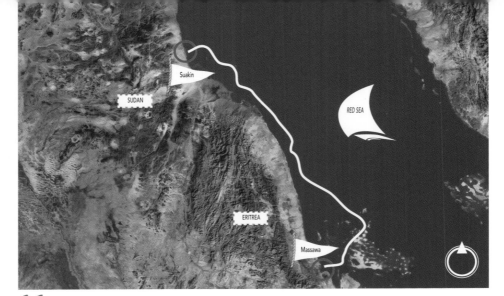

320 Miles. Three days. The city, once rich and wonderful, was eroded by desert winds that transformed the coral buildings into a spectral and evocative setting of ghostly arabesques.

Suakin

A DESERTED DESERT CITY

We navigate the very narrow passage, we graze past a bend then another and finally we encounter an incredible sight – a small and perfectly round islet where the channel ends and forks. On the island, there is a city with towers, porticos, mosques, and large gateways protected by cannons. There is little space to anchor, so little that we have to use two anchors, one at the prow, the other at the stern, facing a stone arch that constitutes the northern entrance to the city. This is probably how merchant ships anchored when they arrived here.

Once on land, to enter the city we have to push through a gigantic creaking gate that seems like it is going to fall to pieces. Just a few steps and we are in a ghostly world. There are abandoned, half-collapsing buildings, circling vultures emitting sharp cries, and eddies of sand that the whistling wind blows from one area of ruins to another. This is what remains of Suakin, once one of the most flourishing ports on the Red Sea. Gold was traded here as well as ivory, spices, and ostrich feathers. There was once a significant slave market here, too. The inhabitants were rich, they built palaces and other buildings with coral but designed them like those in Venice and Constantinople, embellishing them with arches, wrought iron, cupolas, and colored tiles. Then suddenly everything stopped. Ships became too large for the small channel, Port Sudan was built, and Suakin was left abandoned. Sand carried by the wind eroded the buildings over time and they began to collapse, piece by piece, but the grandeur of this place is still evident.

Walking among the debris and rubble, we can still make out the minaret of the large mosque, the columns of the governor's palace, and the gateway to the covered market. We make our way among stumps of arches, skeletons of fences and gates, remnants of steps, and we cross over thresholds into nothingness on the other side. When the sun lowers over the desert and the moon rises over the sea, the sky beyond the ruined coral buildings turns a dark blue. Over Suakin, the clouds pass quickly blown by the wind and moving shadows animate the ancient structures in a play of arabesques and lace patterns. The decaying minaret seems to move back and forth, and an invisible hand continually opens and closes the entrance to the arcade bordering the dock with storage areas for spices. Legend has it that ancient inhabitants of Suakin still return here on nights with a full moon to have fun in the old buildings. It could be the wind that blows incessantly, it could be the tide that beats against the shores, but we sense the sounds of muffled voices speaking in the guttural and aspirate inflections of Arabic dialects.

276 bottom Among the debris and rubble, you can still make out the minaret at the large mosque, the columns at the governor's palace, and the portal to the covered market.

277 One anchor at the prow and another at the stern, facing the stone arch that acted as the entrance to the city, is probably how old ships anchored here.

Suakin

278-279 We sail along the very narrow inlet, graze past a bend then another, and finally the incredible appears: a perfectly round islet where the waterway ends and forks, embracing this city island of towers, porticos, mosques, and large gateways protected by cannons. Suakin was once the most flourishing port on the coast.

279 Sand carried by the wind has eroded the buildings over time and, piece by piece, they have crumbled, but the grandeur of this place is still evident. A legend says that the inhabitants of ancient Suakin return here on nights with a full moon to play among the old abandoned buildings.

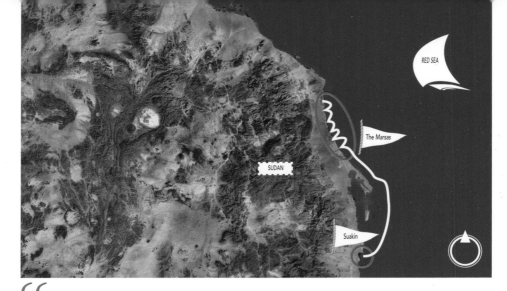

" 200 Miles. The marsas are turquoise watery ribbons that poke into the desert, arid coastline, with its rocks bleached by the sun, some camels, and very few inhabitants to enjoy this rugged yet marvelous landscape. "

The Marsas

PORTS ON THE RED SEA

The African coast of the Red Sea is punctuated with *marsas*. These are natural ports, solitary inlets, slotted into the desert, where we could stay for months before anyone noticed we were here. Perhaps, they are the remains of rivers that disappeared centuries ago or maybe ancient cracks in the earth's surface through which sea water poured. For us, they are precious refuges that allow us to anchor the boat, sheltered from the ever-present headwinds in this spectacular region.

Entering a *marsa* is always a delicate task. You must navigate by sight and guesstimate your path through coral outcrops battered by breakers, but once inside you find a kind of calm and a deep waterway that ends in a small saltwater lake. There is nothing around us except barren banks, hills, and the wind, of course. Every once in a while, a cloud of dust in the distance reveals the passage of camels and Bedouins moving along the ancient caravan track that connects Egypt

with Sudan. At the Arakiai *marsa*, however, we encounter military personnel at a meager encampment of just a few tents, a hut, and one pack of camels. It is past afternoon when we notice the soldiers and the sun is now too low on the horizon to change course and leave. We confine ourselves to anchoring away from land hoping to remain unobserved. Unwritten rules say that where there are military forces, it's better not to disembark on land. It is also not very clear whether a sailboat is permitted to stop in the Sudanese *marsas* after leaving Port Sudan, or in Egyptian *marsas* before making an official entrance into Egypt, so everyone suggests staying off the coast for security reasons. We stick to that advice and remain in the boat under cover as we begin to hear whistling and calls from the shore. We look through the porthole and see men in rolled-up trousers advancing through the water to within a few yards of the boat, waving their arms to get our attention. This goes on until sunset but we continue to ignore them.

The next morning when we rise from our berths we become aware of something heading straight for us. It is an ugly wooden boat with a half dozen soldiers on board, paddling with two different kinds of oars and apparently not that familiar with how to use them. They proceed with great deal of effort because of the headwind and overloaded boat, but proceed they do. We can do nothing other than watch their comical yet worrying behavior and then help them come aboard. We already think we'll have to show our papers and provide a mountain of explanations, but they just seem to want to ask us some urgent questions, some in English and some in Arabic: "How much time have you been at sea? Do you need water or bread?" They then unload onto our deck two cans of fresh water and a bag of their gray-colored flatbread, still warm. During our whole voyage, we have never felt so narrow-minded and so stupid for having blindly listened to the advice of overanxious people.

280 bottom The African coast on the Red Sea is punctuated by marsas, natural ports, inlets slotted into the desert where you can stay for months before anyone even notices you're there.

281 For those navigating towards the Suez Canal, the marsas are precious refuges that allow you to anchor and rest, sheltered from the perennial headwinds in this spectacular sea.

The Marsas

282 Entering the marsas is always a delicate task as you must navigate by sight with the sun behind you and guesstimate your path among coral outcrops battered by the breakers.

282-283 Once past the outcrops at the entrance, you find yourself on a sort of calm and deep river, which ends in a small, saltwater lake with barren shores, hills, and all the while the wind, of course.

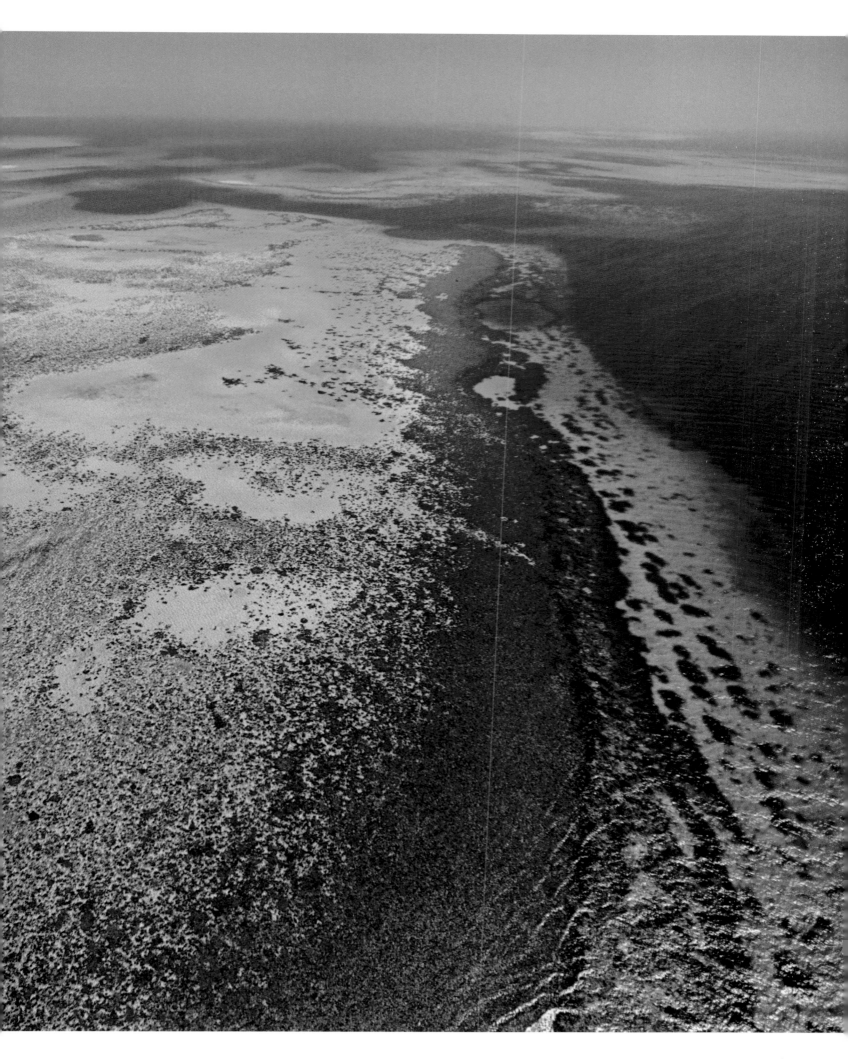

284-285 The coral reef prevents anyone from getting too near the coastline, so you must anchor at a distance and wait for an opportunity to disembark in a dinghy.

284 bottom Beyond the reef, the lagoon water provides beautiful light blues that contrast with the rugged but desolate beauty of this island.

285 bottom On shore, we see only bleached and calcified sea turtle shells and the only sound is that of the wind whistling among the old limestone peaks.

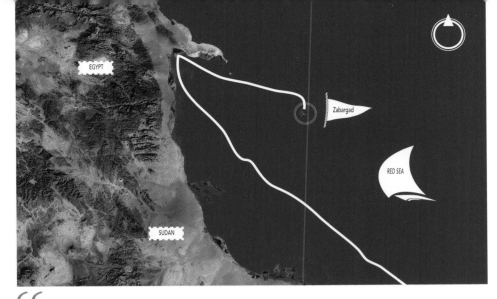

" 180 Miles. Four more days of navigation in headwinds and then,
if time permits, we'll anchor on the leeward side of an uninhabited
island that may still hide an ancient treasure trove. "

Zabargad

THE ISLAND OF THE OLIVINE

Zabargad rises up in the middle of the Red Sea, alone and forgotten, but it is Egyptian territory and you need a special permit to go there, so special that getting it is an adventure in itself. We present ourselves to all the appropriate authorities, including the navy, the police, and customs officials, who all confine themselves to saying: "It's prohibited, but upon request, you may go there." We can't understand why they are so concerned about going to such a distant and barren island.

At dawn, after a long and tiring sail, Zabargad looks like a cream puff dusted with cocoa. The wind blows incessantly for 12 months of the year and has stripped the land of vegetation, leaving only rocks and golden sand below, and sun-scorched brown rock formations above. Disembarking is difficult. Zabargad is surrounded by a coral reef that prevents anyone from getting too near the coastline. We anchor with difficulty a great distance from land and approach in our dinghy. Once we pass the coral reef, we enter a lagoon, the water suddenly becomes calm and the dark blue of the sea transforms into a soft azure color. We sail over a seabed not quite 7 ft (2 m) beneath us, over light-colored sand that stunningly highlights the fish and coral in this absolutely uncontaminated environment. Zabargad is so distant from the coast that few tourists come here, and because of the incessant winds and waves of the Red Sea it is protected even from local fishermen. Consequently, its coral reef has remained intact.

The lagoon water has magnificent colors that starkly contrast with the beautiful but nevertheless desolate landscape. On shore, there are only sea turtle shells and whalebones now bleached and calcified by the sun. The only sound is that of the wind whistling around the ancient pinnacles of limestone. We climb up the sloping hills where chrysolite, a green mineral with the common name of olivine, similar to emerald, was mined in the time of the pharoahs. Our information says that one of the mines should still be accessible. To get there we have to climb up the mountain against the steadily increasing winds that seem to carry more and more sand. After rounding countless rocky outcrops, a black round eye appears, piercing the sun-scorched mountainside. It is the entrance to the mine. Our information indicates that entry is dangerous and the more than 3,000-year-old quarry could collapse solely from the vibrations of our footsteps. But we are here now. We crouch down, advancing slowly, immersed in darkness, but finally we are out of the wind. When our eyes get used to the dark, we can distinguish a myriad of reflections that appear here and there on the walls. By the light of our flashlight, we can clearly see gleaming crystals in the rock. Going further inside the belly of the mountain, we can even see flashes of light in the black dust through which we tread. They are the same flashes of light that fascinated the pharaohs and the ancient Egyptians more than 2,000 years ago.

286-287 Leaving the Suez Canal, it takes two days of sailing and one night anchored in the acrid lakes of Al-Ismaelia City to reach Port Said and we return to the world we know.

286 bottom Out of Suez, it seems as though we're sailing through sand, surrounded as we are by the beige desert, the sun reflecting in every single grain.

287 bottom Boats waiting to pass through the canal are anchored at the dock, just a few dozen yards from ships sailing past a background of minarets.

" 50 Miles. Our last six days of headwinds and at last the Red Sea narrows like a funnel and we breathe a sigh of relief. We are at the southern entrance to the Suez Canal. "

The Suez Canal

SHIPS IN THE DESERT

The last 10 miles (16 km) of the Gulf of Suez are dramatic, with a headwind and an incredible amount of shipping entering and exiting the canal. The unexpected siege of transit agents just adds to this drama. There is an agent to perform all of the local Arabic procedures required to get the permission to navigate this canal through the middle of the desert to Port Said. There are also agents who will secure the same documentation on behalf of their clients. They lie in wait just a few miles from the Suez Canal, keeping an eye out for approaching craft and vying with each other to intercept them first. Once they sight us, they launch into their badgering routine, with one latching onto the gunwale shouting his name and fee as we attempt to maneuver among the waves and handle the wind without colliding with the next agent waiting to accost us if at all possible. Once we arrive at the Suez dock where sailboats must anchor, the agents present themselves again, each one with a small gift like a small baguette, a package of sweets, or a bouquet of flowers as if to gain pardon for previously accosting us at sea. We choose the one offering bread! It takes a week to complete all the required paperwork and meanwhile we remain moored in the midst of the ancient city, watching ships pass just a few yards from us against a background of minarets and mosques. Then one morning, the moment arrives when we can also set off on our way to the Mediterranean.

Our pilot rises before dawn and quickly initiates a litany of incessant requests geared at obtaining, as gifts, the largest number of items possible, from the bar of soap he catches a glimpse of in the galley to an illustrated magazine for his wife, from a sweater for his mother to a cap for his father. Additionally, he wants to know what *baksheesh* (tip or bribe) we might give him at the end of the day, just in recompense for his ability to take advantage of every occasion to raise the ante. It takes two days to reach Port Said and for two days the pilot continues to ask patiently, waiting for a response then with incessant and

exasperating repetition. Apart from the pilot, our days through the canal are a timeless and surreal period, surrounded by an ancient and lunar landscape. It seems as though we're sailing through sand, surrounded as we are so closely by the beige desert with the sun reflected in every single grain.

The canal is a purplish black ribbon of water. Ships of every type come up alongside us, follow behind, and precede us: enormous oil tankers, gigantic container ships, ocean liners with six decks that are really floating hotels, *feluccas* full of packaged bolts of fabric, beat-up fishing boats, and pilot service vessels. There is a section where convoys proceed in two lanes, two strips of water, each not much wider than a ship, separated by a series of sand dunes. On these sections, the ships passing us appear to be mirages moving through the sand. Until the end of the 1800s camel caravans passed through this same region, the true ships of the desert moving across this short stretch of land connecting the Indian Ocean to the Mediterranean Sea. After one night anchoring in the glistening black and acrid lakes of Al-Ismaelia City and another day of slowly sliding through the desert, we see Port Said and we return to the sounds and sights of what we call the civilized world.

> *450 Miles. Four days. We're back in the Mediterranean Sea with its light and unreliable winds, and intense traffic that doesn't allow for any distractions.*

Rhodes

REENTERING CIVILIZATION

Wow, we aren't used to this anymore! Since we first left the Mediterranean, apart from a couple of times in an emergency, we had never been able to get so close to a wharf. We are now entering the Rhodes port via a waterway that says it is home to the feet of the Giant (from *The Colossus of Rhodes*, directed by Sergio Leone in 1961) and we find ourselves looking at a spectacle that we had forgotten. On our left, dozens of

sailboats are lined up alongside the quay, all with their anchors dropped in the middle of the port, their sterns against the wharf and fenders pressed together, side by side. We will never be able to fit inside this configuration of boats! There really isn't any space left! However, just like getting on to a seemingly packed and crowded train, where there are 100 boats there is still room for one more, and so a miracle happens and we are able to wedge in between two boats. "Just one hour later and you would not have been able to moor here, at least not without a reservation!" was the comment of a neighboring mariner. This has also not happened to us in a long time.

We are here at the height of the summer season. There is a swarm of crews all around us loading baggage and stowing enormous quantities of food, though they will be in another port in just a couple of days where they can purchase the same things. The boats are extremely clean, equipped with all of the latest accessories and every convenience possible, and also larger and more luxurious than our own. Our sail bags are faded and discolored, one stay repaired as well as possible with a line and clamps, the keel is dirty, and the flag is a bit frayed. We look like someone's poor relations ourselves. On the other hand, we are the only boat to have a wind rudder.

On the opposite side of the wharf is the promenade with the noise and fumes from cars, and a series of tourist stores and bars where from sunset they will start drinking *ouzo*, continuing all evening and throughout the night enjoying food and music. We cannot ignore our return to civilization, both ancient and modern. We savor only what is necessary of it and the time it takes to get our paperwork in order, buy water and fuel, take advantage of a laundromat and restaurant then leave again. However, not before calling the port diver to free our anchor, which in not more than 24 hours, is inextricably buried beneath a tangle of chains.

288 center The Green Boat's sails are ruffled, one stay has been repaired as well as it can be, and its keel is dirty, yet undoubtedly this boat has sailed further than all the others docked here at the port.

288 bottom Mediterranean ports are always incredibly crowded, but you must enter and find a spot to drop anchor. It is sometimes even more stressful than making a crossing.

288-289 Entering the port of Mandraky at Rhodes, we pass by a channel that says it accommodates one of the Giant's feet (from The Colossus of Rhodes, directed by Sergio Leone in 1961).

289 bottom It always looks like there won't be an anchorage but in the end one is found. Where 100 boats can fit, so can 101!

Rhodes

290 After the thousands of miles between the arid desert shores of the Red Sea, country wildflowers quench your eyes like crystal-clear water quenches a dry, thirsty throat.

291 top and bottom right Following the loss of Christian territories in the Holy Land, an order of the Knights of Malta took refuge in Rhodes and the ruins of their castles still stand here today.

291 bottom left After so many miles on distant yet spectacular, unfamiliar yet warm seas, here is the Mediterranean again, familiar and always benevolent.

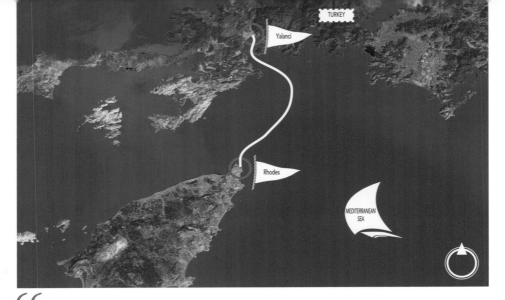

> 30 Miles. It only takes a few hours to go from Arabic narrow and closely intertwined lanes to Greek classic architecture, and then on to Asian bazaars.

Marmaris

LIFE IN A SHIPYARD

The southwest coast of Turkey is one of the few places in the Mediterranean where nature still resists and persists. The scents of resin from the pine forests waft down as far as the sea, deep-water bays, and miles of uninhabited coastline. There are only a few, very small towns, with narrow streets paved in ancient stone. The place where we stop is called Yalanci Bogaz, located on an isthmus south of Marmaris. We have to clean up the keel and put our boat back in order as it has been damaged by years in the sun, the wind carrying sand from the Red Sea, and by the thousands of miles of ocean we have traveled. There is a shipyard here where they repair wooden kayaks and some

American and Australian sailboats that, after going through the Red Sea, are being put back in order before confronting the Mediterranean and the Atlantic. The small city of Marmaris is just a few miles away but the road there has no surface and the minibus shuttling between here and there takes almost an hour. At least we have once again successfully found an isolated place.

We have to desalinate and bareboat the fiberglass hull, and apply a new protective coating to it. It is a dirty job carried out in the dust and smoke of resin, made all the more arduous when the temperature rises above 86°. To add the new resin layer we get up at four in the morning, work until the sun is at its peak and it begins to get hot. Then we take care of other smaller repairs. There are nine shipyard workers and right from the start they treat us as if we've always been a part of their team. At mid-morning and mid-afternoon, one of them prepares an enormous kettle of tea and passes it around in glasses. At midday, we gather in the large hut to eat together. They make tomatoes with onions and parsley, fried eggplant, and pies with ground meat, potatoes, and peppers. On Saturday when we work only until lunchtime, we cook. Macaroni with tuna and tomatoes is well received by everyone.

The most enjoyable ritual is the one that occurs at five o'clock in the evening. The men stop working, wash up, and sit with us, all looking out to sea. The shipyard master comes by with a cupful of *raki* and pours a finger into each of our 11 glasses then fills them up with really cold water. The strong dry milky liquid with the flavor of anise relaxes our bodies and our souls. The setting sun lights up their faces, with their dark green eloquent eyes, eyes that together with hands and a few English words are the means by which these nine people communicate, telling us about their children, families, and work.

292 bottom and 293 bottom Roasted by the sun, blasted by the wind carrying sand on the Red Sea, battered by oceanic waves, and thousands of miles traveled, the Green Boat needs some TLC.

292-293 We sail for miles along an uninhabited coast that, from time to time, comes to life with the presence of country folk in old villages paved with ancient stone.

294-295 The southwestern coast of Turkey is one of the few places in the Mediterranean where nature still resists and persists with the scents from the pine forests wafting down to the sea and deep water bays.

296-297 In the midst of the Adriatic, the sea is still overcrowded and you must remain in the cockpit during downpours, keeping an eye out for boats that might cross your path too closely.

296 bottom Dubrovnik, or Ragusa, as the Greeks named it, was the fifth Italian Marine Republic and is a UNESCO World Heritage Site.

297 bottom With this improbable craft, Vladimir has navigated from Crimea to Greece, Albania, Croatia, and at dawn he left Dubrovnik for Italy.

298-299 Legend says that when God created the world, he cast a handful of stones out into the sea, forming the islands of the Kornati Archipelago.

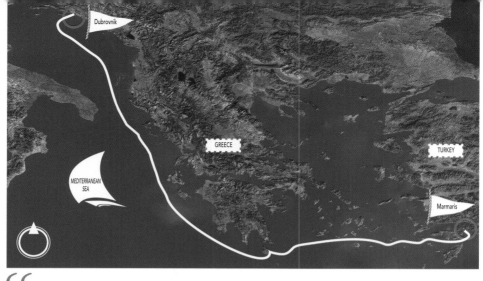

" *950 Miles. For one or two weeks now we have been passing by countless islands rich in history.* "

Dubrovnik

THERE'S ROOM FOR ALL KINDS AT SEA

It has been a difficult night of storms, low winds, and rain. In the ocean, we would have lowered the sails and spent the night in our berth, waiting for better weather. Here in the middle of the Adriatic, however, the sea is too crowded to allow ourselves the luxury of not standing guard. So we take turns staying outside through the black and rainy night, attempting to stay at full sail, making our way towards Dubrovnik while keeping an eye out for the lights of any ships that may appear and disappear behind the downpours. By dawn we are soaked to the bone, the wind has completely died down, and we start thinking that if we want to get to Dubrovnik by evening, we'd better give in and start the engine.

While contemplating what to do, a small sailboat appears just a few degrees portside. At first we think perhaps it is a boat many miles away with its hull still hidden beneath the horizon, but looking at it through our binoculars the sail seems strangely like that of a windsurfer! We start our engine and head for this strange object in the distance. After a while, the hull appears and is even stranger than the sail. The craft has a structure similar to a dinghy with a mast and mainsail. It also has a tiny jib and there's a person standing on this watercraft of sorts, gesticulating. Is it a shipwrecked person that needs help? The distance between us decreases, while the small man also maneuvers to make his way towards us. At just over 100 yards (90 m) away he disappears under some sort of covering and reappears after just a few seconds with a camera. So he doesn't need our assistance after all! His craft is constructed out of two rubber dinghy inner tubes held together with a rigid platform not much wider than the floor of a ridge tent. A 16- to 20-ft (5–6-m) mast with a converted windsurfing sail stands at the prow. "I'm Vladimir," the occupant introduces himself, "please, do you know my coordinates?" A very elegant way to ask, "Where in the hell am I?" We tell him that we are 15 miles (24 km) southwest of Dubrovnik, but that isn't enough for him. He disappears and reappears again with his nautical map, actually a highway map stretching from Greece to Italy, asking us to mark our location on it.

Vladimir is a Russian who began his voyage in the Crimea, sailed to Greece, headed up the coasts of Albania and Croatia, stopped for three days in Dubrovnik, and this morning was heading towards Italy. "The rain surprised me and now I don't know which route I've traveled!" He doesn't seem worried about the crossing he has yet to confront but is in a real hurry to get going again. "It would be best if you'd tell me how to get to the other side." He takes one last picture, thanks us, hoists the sails, allows them to catch the wind, and goes on his way. We see him move away like an archangel on an unlikely watercraft, demonstrating once again that there's room for all kinds at sea.

" *300 Miles. Our last three days of sailing then we return home and begin to tell our story, recount our memories, and plan for the next time out.* "

Venice
RETURNING HOME

300 center Things that we have been used to seeing since childhood come back into view, buildings, stairways, churches, and we can already distinguish the silhouette of San Marco's bell tower in the background.

300 bottom Vaporetti water taxis make scheduled stops at jetties,

unloading and loading, departing again in the constant comings and goings of people who live and work in this living museum.

300-301 Two labyrinths: one on land and another by sea that blend together to form the most magical city in the world, Venice.

We are now just a few miles away, the prow heading straight ahead as we enter the *bocca degli Alberoni*, our last entry to a lagoon on our world tour in a sailboat. Through habit, now instinctive, our eyes scan forward beyond the prow, in search of shadows from coral reefs and other hidden dangers. But we really no longer have to do this. Although the water is green, although we can't see the seabed, we are safe here along one of the most well-traveled and best-marked routes in the world, navigated for centuries by thousands of ships, sailboats, and galleys.

We both turn to look astern. Behind us, the wake of our passage through the entrance grows smaller and in the distance, the azure strip of seawater begins to fade. More distant still is an opaque and blurry horizon now forever hiding that incredible world that for years was our home, those beautiful yet mighty oceans, those thousands of islands, white beaches, smiling people, our 40,000 miles (64,000 km) of life in the middle of the sea … Unfortunately, there is just a muddy channel in front of us that leads towards the inevitable termination of our voyage. But an end there must be and this is certainly the best that anyone could hope for, because beyond the last strip of sand the most beautiful and one of the oldest landing sites in the world beckons. The magnificent profile of San Marco, superb patrician homes with stairways descending to the water, the Grand Canal and the canal of Giudecca, wooden oars and moorings all speaking of the glorious past, momentous history, and culture. Among so much pomp, splendor, and magic, we choose to spend the last night of our voyage anchored in a small channel behind Torcello. It is a green place, solitary and silent with cloudy water, the scents from Venetian squares and the sea blending together in the air without one prevailing over the other, as if the wind wants to harmonize our hearts and souls, balancing us somewhere between the desire to get back on terra firma and the wish to go back out to sea.

AUTHORS

Elisabetta Eördegh and **Carlo Auriemma** have been voyaging round the world by sailing boat since 1988. After a first three-year-long circumnavigation, they fitted out their vessel, *Barca Pulita* (Clean Boat), an ecological and eco-friendly sailing boat, and since 1993 have been exploring the oceans in search of the world's last pristine corners. Meanwhile, they founded the Barca Pulita Association (Clean Boat Association), whose members aim to document and protect these imperilled regions. Over the years Elisabetta Eördegh and Carlo Auriemma have published Sotto un grande cielo (Under a big sky) with Mursia; *Mar d'Africa* (Sea of Africa) with Feltrinelli; and *Partire* (Leaving), with Editrice Incontri Nautici. They have also produced a series of TV documentaries on the world's more remote and less known natural and anthropological areas.

INDEX

c = caption

A
Aden, port of, 260, 261c
Adriatic Sea, 296c, 297
Afar Tribe, 267
Africa, 40, 237c, 239c, 242, 243c, 244c, 250, 256c, 267, 273
Aitutaki, island, 76
Albania, 296c, 297
Alberoni, bocca degli, 300
Alboran Sea, 39
Aldabra Island, 228, 228c
Alghero, 32
Al-Ismaelia City, 286c
Ambrym, bay, volcano, island, 130c, 131
American Samoa, 97
Anak Krakatoa, island, 13, 182, 183c
Andaman Islands, 13, 18c, 203, 207
Antilles, islands, 40, 56
Anuta, island, 13, 135
Apia, port, 97, 98c, 100c
Arabian Peninsula, 239c, 244c
Arakiai Marsa, 280
Asia, 207, 273
Asmara, 273
Atlantic Ocean, 38c, 40, 49, 62, 292
Atolls of the Phoenix, 13, 106c, 107, 109c
Atuona Bat, 80
Australia, 14, 18c, 148, 153, 166
Ayu, 13

B
Bab-el-Mandeb, 262c, 263c
Baie des Verges, 80, 81c
Baie des Vierges, 80, 81c
Balearic Islands, 32
Bali, island, 13, 178, 179c
Bay of Bengal, 203, 207
Beira, 236, 237c
Benoa, port of, 178
Bocca di Magra, 22
Bora Bora, island, 76, 88, 90c, 91c
Bora Bora, lagoon, 90c
Borneo, island, 13, 184c, 185, 188c
Botany Bay, 145
Bramble Cay lighthouse, 153
Bridge of the Americas, 62
Brunei, 184c
Burma, 198c, 199

C
Cala Maestra, 26c, 27
California, 118
Calpe, 38c
Calvi, 28, 29c
Canal Grande, 300
Canaries, islands, 40, 41c, 43c
Canton Island, 107
Cape Corsica, 28
Cape Horn, 62
Caribbean, 56, 57c
Central America, 9
Chagos Islands, 13, 18, 218, 219c
Chole Island, 238
China, 197
Cinque Terre, 22
Cocos Island, 65, 66c
Colombia, 16, 56
Colon, port of, 62
Colosso di Rodi, 288, 289c
Cook Islands, 92c, 93
Cook's Bay, 89c
Corsica, island, 28c
Cosmoledo, island, 228, 228c
Costa Rica, 65, 66c
Constantinople, 276
Crater, 260, 261c
Crimea, 296c, 297
Croatia, 296c, 297

D
Dahlak Archipelago, 18, 268c, 270c, 273
Dahlak Kebir, 267
Dar es Salaam, 238, 242
Darwin, 153, 164, 165c, 166
Denpasar Airport, 178
Diego Garcia, island, 218
Dubrovnik (Ragusa), 296c, 297

E
Ecuador, 69
Egypt, 267, 280
Eritrea, 18, 262c, 263, 267, 270c, 273
Ethiopia, 270c
Europe, 40, 88, 89c, 148, 192, 207

F
Farquhar Atoll, lagoon, 228, 228c, 231c
Fatu Hiva, island of, 80, 81c
Fiascherino, 22
Fijian islands, 16, 116c, 118, 123, 123c
Formentera, island, 34, 36c
France, 14, 18c, 28
French Polynesia, 88, 89c
Funafuti, 110, 110c

G
Galapagos Islands, 13, 68c, 69, 70c, 72c, 76
Galle, port at, 206c, 207, 207c
Galliard Cut, 62, 63c
Gan, island, 219c
Gatun Lake, 62
George Town, 194
Gibraltar, 13, 14, 38c, 39
Gibraltar, lighthouse on, 38c
Giudecca, canal of, island of, 300, 300c
Gran Roque, island, 55c
Great Barrier Reef, 145
Greece, 296c, 297
Guadalcanal, 76
Gulf of Poets, 22
Gulf of Suez, 287

H
Hadiboo, village of, 255
Hanish Islands, 18, 262c, 263
Hermit Islands, 142
Hiva Hoa, bay at, 80
Holy Land, 291c
Honiara, 141
Horn of Africa, 18
Humboldt Current, 70c

I
Ibiza, island, 34, 35c
India, 203, 210, 213c, 267
Indian Ocean, 13, 18c, 153, 182, 207, 218, 260, 263, 287
Indonesia, 154, 176, 192, 238
Irian Jaya, 154, 156
Italy, 16, 32, 103, 123, 296c, 297

J
Japan, 107, 154
Java, island, 182
Java Sea, 182, 185

K
Kalimantan (Indonesia), 184c
Kaprus, village of, 154c
Kapuas River, 13, 185
Kenya, 250
Kilifi, fjord at, 250, 251c
Kiribati, 107
Kochi, lagoon, 210, 211c
Komodo, archipelago, 172c, 173, 174c
Korea, 107
Kornati Archipelago, 296c
Krakatoa, island, volcano, 182, 183c
Kyoto Protocol, 110

L
La Digue, island of, 224c
La Gomera, island of, harbor at, 40, 43c
Lamalera, 13, 168, 171c
Langkawi Archipelago, 193c
Latam, island of, 13, 249
Le Grazie, 22
Lembata, island of, 168
Lenakel, 126c
Lerici, 22
Los Gigantes, bay of, 40
Los Roques, archipelago of, 50, 52c

M
Madagascar, island, 13, 18, 232
Mafia Island, 238, 239c
Magra, port of, 22
Mahatma Gandhi Marine National Park, 202c

Mahé, 224c
Majorca, island, 34
Maketi Fou, market, 100c
Malaysia, 185, 192, 198c, 199
Maldives, islands, 13, 18, 213c, 215c, 219c, 225
Malé, 212, 216
Malindi, 251c
Mandraky, port of, 289c
Marmaris, city of 292
Marovo, lagoon, of, 141
Marquesas, islands, 76, 80, 81c, 85, 88
Massawa, 272c, 273, 274c
Mauritius, island, 218
Mecca, 273, 274c
Mediterranean Sea, 13, 14, 18, 27, 32, 36c, 38c, 39, 242, 243c, 287, 288, 289c, 291c, 292, 293c
Melville, island, 13, 166
Minorca, island, 32, 34
Moka, 263
Moluccas, islands, 161
Monastery, The, 26c, 27
Monte Cristo, 27
Moorea, island, 88, 89c
Morgan's Head, 56, 57c
Mount Mahon, 32
Mount Vaea, 97
Mozambique, 13, 236, 237c
Mozambique Channel, 232c, 235c, 236

N
New Panganga Bay, 196c, 197
Niuatoputapu, 102c, 103, 104c
Nosy Komba, island, 232, 235c
Nukufetau, atoll of, 110c
Nuku Hiva, island, 80
Nusa Tenggara, islands, 168
Nusalembongans, island, 176, 177c

P
Pacific Ocean, 13, 62, 76, 77c, 80, 97, 107, 110, 116c, 123, 153, 238
Palmaria, 22
Palos, 40
Panama, 13, 14, 56, 57c, 58, 59c, 62, 65, 68c
Panama Canal, 62, 63c, 190
Papeete, island, 88, 89c
Papua New Guinea, 142, 150, 153
Penang Island, 194, 195c
Peru, 65
Phuket Island, 197
Pillars of Hercules, 38c, 39
Point Venus, 88
Polynesia, 82c, 103, 153
Pontianak, river port 185
Port Blair, 202c, 203
Port Jackson, 148
Port of Spain, 48c, 49
Porto Venere, 16, 22, 23c
Port Resolution, 126c
Port Said, 286c, 287
Port Sudan, 276, 280
Praslin Island, 225, 227c
Providencia, island, 56, 57c
Puerto Ayora, 68c, 69, 71c
Pulau Jarak, island, 192, 193c

Q
Queensland, 145
Quelelevu, atoll, 13, 114c, 115

R
Raiatea, island, 88, 89c
Rainbow Reef, 119c
Raroia, atoll, 85
Red Sea, 13, 18, 18c, 244c, 260, 262c, 263, 273, 274c, 276, 280, 280c, 285, 287, 291c, 292, 293c
Revellata lighthouse, 29c
Rinca Island, 173
Rhodes, 288, 289c, 291c
Roma Island, 103, 161

S
Salomon Islands Atoll, 218
Samarai Island, 150
Samoa, islands, 97, 98c, 101c, 103, 106c, 107
San Blas Islands, 58, 59c
San Cristobal, island of, 69
Santa Catalina, island, 56
Santa Cruz, island of, 69
Sa Penya, port, 34

Sarad, 267
Sarawak (Malaysia), 184c
Saudi Arabia, 266c, 267, 273
Scotland, 97
Sentinel, island, 203
Seychelles Islands, 224c, 225, 228, 228c, 231c
Siberia, 257c
Singapore, 185, 190, 190c, 192, 238, 263, 264c
Society Islands, 13, 88, 89c, 90c
Socotra, island, 18, 254c, 255, 257c
Solomon Islands, 139, 145
Somalia, 250, 251c, 255
South Bay, 148
South China Sea, 190
South West Bay, 263
Spain, 32, 38c, 39, 118
Spinalunga (Giudecca), island, 300c
Sri Lanka, 18, 206c, 207, 213c
Strait of Bab-el-Mandeb, 263c
Strait of Malacca, 185, 192, 199
Suakin, 276, 278c, 279c
Sudan, 267, 280
Suez Canal, 13, 14, 218, 280c, 286c, 287
Sumatra, island, 182, 185, 192
Sunda Strait, 13
Surin Islands, 199
Suva, 76
Suvarov Atoll, 92c, 93, 95c
Sydney, 148

T
Tafahi, island of, 102c
Tahaa, island, 88, 89c
Tahiti, island, 62, 88
Tanganyika, 247c
Tanna Island, 13, 126c, 127, 128c, 130c
Tanzania, 13, 247c, 250, 251c
Tarawa, 106c, 107
Taulud, island, 272c
Taveuni, island, 118, 119c
Tellaro, 22
Tenerife, island, 40
Thailand, 197, 198c, 199
Thames, river, 39
Tino lighthouse, 22
Tobago, 48c, 49
Tonga, archipelago, 103
Tongatapu, island, 76
Torcello, island 300
Torres Strait, 13, 14, 153
Trinidad and Tobago, 48c, 49
Tuamotu Archipelago, 85, 88
Tulusdoo, island, 212
Tunisia, 28
Turkey, 100, 292, 293c
Tuvalu, islands, country of, 110, 110c, 112c, 113c
Tyrrhenian Sea, 26c, 27

U
United Kingdom, 38c, 39, 218, 222c
United States, 218
Utupua Island, 139

V
Vailima, Villa, village of 97
Vallée de Mai, 225, 227c
Vanguan Island, 141
Vanikoro Island, 139
Vanualevu, island, 119c
Vanuatu, islands, people, 13, 127, 128c, 131
Venice, 276, 300c
Venezuela, 52c, 56, 57c

W
Waiyevo, 118
Western Samoa, 96c, 97, 99c

Y
Yakel, 13, 127, 128c, 129c
Yalanci Bogaz, 292
Yasur, volcano, 126c
Yemen, 255, 260, 262c, 263, 267

Z
Zabargad, island, 285
Zanzibar, island, 18, 242, 243c, 244c, 247c, 249

302

PHOTO CREDITS

ACKNOWLEDGEMENTS

It was wonderful to receive the proposal to write this book from Marcello Bertinetti and equally wonderful, during the writing process, to be monitored, assisted,

and advised by Laura Accomazzo and Valeria Manferto. Additional thanks go to them for restoring our romantic idea of the *editor*.

We are grateful to our friends who accompanied us on shorter or longer voyages, and who also shared their photos with us:

Mauro Antelli, Nives Blasi, Francesco Frongia, Annalisa Lo Sacco, Simona Mosna, Franco Pace, Elena Poto, and Fausto Sassi.

Thanks to our daughters, Margherita and Tessa, for reading and harshly critiquing our drafts.

Although we have traveled in a boat for more than 20 years, we are not yet able to cut the cord that connects us to our home

where without help from many people we could not have taken this spectacular voyage.

Among these, we would like to thank: C. Map, Veco Frigoboat, Libreria del Mare (Maritime Bookstore) of Milan, Valerio Grassi from Seatec,

Salmini Impianti Eolici (Salmini Wind Generators), Lofrans, and On-Air.

And, personal thanks go to:

Alberto Casagrande, Piera Casari, Giorgio Casti, and Carlo Formenti, along with all of the other people that we have not acknowledged here in writing,

yet over the years have given us an infinite amount of assistance, both great and small.

WS White Star Publishers® is a registered trademark
property of De Agostini Libri S.p.A.

© 2009, 2014 De Agostini Libri S.p.A.
Via G. da Verrazano, 15
28100 Novara, Italy
www.whitestar.it - www.deagostini.it

Translation: Erin Jennison

ISBN 978-88-544-0882-1
1 2 3 4 5 6   18 17 16 15 14

Printed in China